SOUNDING THE CLASSICS

SOUNDING THE CLASSICS

From Sophocles to Thomas Mann

RUDOLPH BINION

PRAEGER

Westport, Connecticut
London

The Library of Congress has cataloged the hardcover edition as follows:

Binion, Rudolph, 1927–
    Sounding the classics : from Sophocles to Thomas Mann / Rudolph
Binion.
        p.   cm.—(Contributions to the study of world literature,
    ISSN 0738–9345 ; no. 83)
    Includes bibliographical references and index.
    ISBN 0–313–30458–0 (hc : alk. paper).—ISBN 0–275–95965–1 (pb :
alk. paper)
    1. Fiction—History and criticism. I. Title. II. Series.
    PN3353.B56 1997   97–1693

British Library Cataloguing in Publication Data is available.

A hardcover edition of *Sounding the Classics* is available from Greenwood Press,
an imprint of Greenwood Publishing Group, Inc. (Contributions to the Study
of World Literature, Number 83; ISBN 0–313–30458–0).

Library of Congress Catalog Card Number: 97–1693
ISBN: 0–275–95965–1

First published in 1997

Praeger Publishers, 88 Post Road West, Westport, CT 06881
An imprint of Greenwood Publishing Group, Inc.

Printed in the United States of America

The paper used in this book complies with the
Permanent Paper Standard issued by the National
Information Standards Organization (Z39.48–1984).

10 9 8 7 6 5 4 3 2 1

Copyright Acknowledgments

SOUNDING THE CLASSICS

1

Text and Subtext

Why do most readers at most times and places find a certain few works of literature great? At least since Aristotle the answer has been sought in the West in such textual qualities as plot, style, or argument. I propose to seek it instead in the interplay of two aspects of any literary classic: what it states outright and what it conveys between the lines. More specifically, I mean to explore that interplay in each of a dozen undisputed and broadly representative Western literary classics by turns, casting few glances forward or backward along the way. My final aim is to pool my dozen findings in a general conclusion about what makes a classic a classic.

Let me call the two terms of that interplay "text" and "subtext" for short. In my usage to follow, "text" will denote, then, not just the words comprising a given work, but their overt purport as well. And "subtext" will mean, unsurprisingly, a second understanding of that same work that it itself imparts, only not outright—that it conveys unequivocally, only not immediately or in so many words. Occasional self-explanatory variants such as "overtheme" and "undertheme" will break the monotony of these key terms "text" and "subtext" while also refocusing their meaning as my context may require.

A text is grasped consciously. A subtext is grasped along with a text, but less than consciously unless and until it is searched out or pointed out. Some rough analogies may serve. Hidden-image painting depicts one thing that, as we keep watching it, turns out to contain or to be a second thing as well. This analogy would be exact were trick compositions of the sort also masterworks of painting. But masterworks of painting hardly camouflage alternative images, while conversely even a Degas's dazzling *Steep Coast*, with its mossy hillocks that form a recumbent nude, is no masterwork.[1] Another counterpart in painting to a literary subtext is a symbolic second meaning, as when in the baroque era a flower piece with a falling petal signified to its painter and its viewers alike that life is fleeting. Here the main difference from a subtext or indeed a hidden image is that such a symbolic message was conventional and aboveboard in its time—a leaf, or in this case a petal, from an open book. Ludwig Wittgenstein dismissed the concept of an "inner image" as misleading for some simple line drawings that could equally be seen as either concave or convex and likewise for others that could be taken for either a rabbit's or a duck's head (*Philosophical Investigations*, section 11). His dismissal is weighty because it is his, but it cannot be construed to cover a text and its subtext inasmuch as the subtext is an additional and not an alternative reading. Verbally, a double entendre more closely mimics text and subtext on a small scale except that we do not get the point of it unconsciously before we catch on consciously, or at all odds not much before. By this criterion of catching on unconsciously, a camouflaged hidden image in a painting is closer to a subtext than a double entendre is, visual experimentation having established again and again that we commonly see more than we realize—that we block out collateral perceptions. But the most obvious analogue to text and subtext is a dream, which carries a latent meaning known to the dreamer only unconsciously as a rule. Yet even this analogue in turn falls short, instructively—too instructively indeed for me to take it up before full returns from my dozen texts and subtexts are in.

A dozen seemed to me as many texts and subtexts as readers could bear in mind for the comparative analysis that is my final purpose. I restricted my dozen picks to undisputed classics, thereby avoiding the need to define a classic at the outset, which would have defeated my purpose. I also restricted them to fictional classics (including one fable presented as fact) so as not to have to deal with whether nonfictional classics might be saying what they say only because it legitimately looked right or true: then their subtexts would carry less weight. I excluded pure poetry because its appeal is largely confined to its language of composition. I chose familiar works nearly universally accepted as great in the West (the East is beyond my ken). With just one exception I also chose short works in case a refresher reading were wanted (though I do recap the main story line at the start of each discussion). The single long work I chose is *The Red and the Black*, and this with the excuse that I aimed to represent as many leading literary ages, schools, and traditions as possible and saw no short classic known throughout the West that typifies romanticism quite as well. My chronological cutoff was World War I, for no newer work can be sufficiently sure to endure as by definition classics must. At the same time I chose more and more works toward the end of my chronological line, as ever more fiction has been written and preserved in more modern times. I overrepresented France in the nineteenth century with two works as against none for England, but what possible English substitute for either the Stendhal or the Flaubert is as generally familiar and highly esteemed throughout the West? Hispanophile though I am, I could fit no Spanish classic into my scheme: of even *Don Quixote* hardly more than its pair of protagonists is well known abroad. Accordingly, Shakespeare being a must in any case, I chose *King Lear* instead for that same rich period. No one else's list would likely match mine, but neither should a different romantic or a different Shakespeare affect the end result of the inquiry. My authors include no women, but as authors are not my concern, their sex should not skew my results. Last and least, I privately find one of the works I chose dreadful and only hope that it will not be evident which.

I explore these works successively, each chapter being styled accordingly as the fresh inquiry it was and not as an exposition of its outcome, let alone of its share in my final, composite findings. To have led off each time from foregone conclusions could have made for easier reading, but it would have cast a spurious hue of scheme and system over my exploratory endeavor. Firm leading can be misleading in more ways than one.

Twelve inquiries from scratch topped off by a twelvefold comparison make a hard book to read. Not that I write obscurely: I contrive to say things as simply as they are simple and as clearly as they are clear (more simply or more clearly would be fakery). But my subject itself is dauntingly convoluted and obscure, however easy it may be to state in general terms. In its easiest formulation, that subject is the interrelation of text and subtext, or again the artistic function of subtexts, in Western fiction that has long and widely been seen as great. My basic claim is that such fiction draws its broad and lasting appeal not merely from its express theme, structure, or wording, but equally from that theme's traffic with a second message or meaning conveyed only tacitly. I spell out this subtext of each of my twelve specimen classics and show how it interrelates with their text. I say subtext in the singular advisedly here. Just as a text may sound various themes at once, so may it convey a variety of subthemes. In each of my twelve classics, however, a single express theme predominates even as a single tacit theme holds sway. Not all literary works have running underthemes, but these twelve classics do. Indeed, they are all of a piece textually, with a subtext in tandem from first to last. Such end-to-end doubling is in fact part of what makes a classic a classic, as will emerge in conclusion, when my evidence is all in.

What I identify as the dominant theme of any one of my twelve classics may be questioned. But questioners should not confuse theme with subject. A theme is pitched universally. *King Lear* is about a father's tyrannical doting; its theme, though, is life's shattering turnabouts. *Phaedra* is about a queen's illicit craving; its theme, though, is that sin is irresistible. Underthemes for their part are rarely studied in fiction and never, to my knowledge, for their artistic function. For nonfiction, on the other hand, the notion of an inner or hidden meaning is a commonplace: witness Karl Marx's idea that "ideologies" express class interests in disguise or Leo Strauss's concept of a "writing between the lines" endemic to political philosophy. The pioneering decipherment of a fictional subtext with universal appeal was Freud's reading, or in fact misreading, of *Oedipus the King*, which is why I begin with just that Greek classic rather than with Sophocles' more popular *Antigone* (let alone with my own favorite, *The Bacchae* of Euripides).

But how can I know that I, unlike Freud, am reading straight when I read between the lines of a fictional text—that I am reading out of the work and not into it? This is a double question: of method and of proof. About my method first: I have none. In research, method is for technicians, not for scientists or scholars. It works with databases and black boxes, not sounding lines. Its greatest proponent, René Descartes, achieved none of his insights through its use. New understanding comes of its own, eureka-like, from exhaustive knowledge of a subject and protracted absorption in it. This was Henri Bergson's great lesson, drawn from the history of science. As Bergson explained, the researcher must study a subject outwardly, extrinsically, intellectually, harder and harder until it all at once falls into place around its simple innermost core—or else definitively does not, in which case it is a false entity. My own Bergsonian procedure was to grope for the gist of what each of my twelve classics says outright and of what it says besides, then for how these two gists interrelate in each of them and finally in all twelve alike. It was blindman's buff all the way, even without a blindfold, until at length my texts and subtexts fell into focus each and all.

And how can others now verify that focus into which they fell? The crucial check in each case begins and ends with the subtext: others in turn must see it informing the text from which I infer it and to which I refer it. For this, note well, they must look with open eyes and minds, not with literalist blinders such that they honestly can't see. Once the subtexts are spotted—some close to the text itself, others deep-buried—the question of their artistic function is less intuitive, more analytical. It will arise in the course of the individual studies, but can be answered only tentatively before the comparative analysis saved for the end. If after this comparative analysis any of the connections drawn look or feel forced, they are; if not, they hold. What further verification could be wanted?

Two final prefatory points. First, one and only one of my twelve classics is so styled that its author's personal relation to it is part and parcel of its claim to fame: Goethe's *Werther*. So for the rest I eschew biography in my analysis. And second, Freud gets due mention from me for his theory of latent meaning in *Oedipus the King* and, at my conclusion stage, in fiction generally, but extra mention too in between because my reinterpretation of *Oedipus the King* left me unable to call the Oedipus complex by that name in picking it out of the old Tristan legend. In this fix, what else could I call it as short and clear as "the Freudian complex"?

I used whatever suitable English editions of my eleven non-English classics I could find and, for the rest, translated anew. For the whole scheme of my book, my one conscious debt to a predecessor is to Erich Auerbach: his monumental *Mimesis*, which analyzes period texts in their cultural and social contexts, was for me not a model (its aim is not to define a classic), but an inspiration. Fortunately I need not review the voluminous scholarly literature on each of my classics, as I approach them all quite differently. I must nonetheless have drawn on secondary sources more than my meager notes acknowledge, but to my shame I do not remember which or where. By contrast, I can and now eagerly do credit my several patient helpers with this project from its slow conception to its slower completion. The chapter on *Oedipus the King* originated in a discussion with Monette Vacquin, that on *King Lear* in one with Jacqueline Hecht, and that on the Gospel of Matthew in one with Mike McDuffee; only thereafter did my plan to analyze a dozen classics comparatively as to text and subtext begin to form. I was assisted with Sophocles' Greek usage by Christine Fouché-Friedel and Leonard Muellner, with the biblical backdrop to Matthew by Richard A. Webster, with the iconography of the massacre of the innocents by Caroline Fisher, with Tristan's kinship by Georges Duby, and with Racine's use of Boileau by Murray Sachs. Sean Wilder read my Sophocles in draft, Robert Szulkin my Dostoyevsky, Robert Aldrich my Flaubert, Edward Engelberg my Mann, and Samuel K. Cohn my Tristan and my Francesca. Alice Binion, Deborah Hayden, and Jane Kamensky scrutinized the whole emergent manuscript chapter by chapter, relentlessly critiquing and querying, demanding clarifications and amplifications well beyond my powers; to them my debt is inexpressible.

NOTE

1. See Martin Bailey, "Edgar Degas's Last Years: Making Art That Danced," *Smithsonian* 27, no. 7 (October 1996): 98–100.

2

The Trouble with Oedipus
Sophocles' *Oedipus the King*

This first study will at least begin uncontroversially by restating what everyone already knows about Freud and his favorite Greek tragedy, *Oedipus the King*, composed by Sophocles soon after 430 B.C. This is that Freud considered Sophocles' dramatization of the Oedipus legend to hold a special, enduring fascination because Sophocles' Oedipus, like his legendary prototype, kills his father and marries his mother despite his efforts to elude this fate once it is prophesied for him by an oracle. In so doing, Oedipus acts out, in Freud's famous interpretation, the desire that climaxes every son's early childhood: to possess the mother, who is a son's first sexual object, and to kill the father, who impedes the son's access to her.

Undeniably, Sophocles' *Oedipus the King* held a special, enduring fascination for Freud himself because of Oedipus's fate. Yet Freud's construction on that dramatic masterwork is untenable. For one thing, *Oedipus the King* has engaged the rest of Sophocles' posterity no more than have any number of other ancient Greek tragedies about horrific fates far removed from that of Oedipus; to stick with Sophocles' own works, his *Antigone*, though less finely crafted, outstrips his *Oedipus the King* in continuing popularity even with no father complex showing in its martyred heroine. For another, Sophocles' *Oedipus the King* is not about its hero fulfilling his fate despite all his efforts to elude it, indeed through those very efforts to elude it. Fate has already played its trick on

Oedipus long years before that play begins, as every Athenian spectator knew in advance and no doubt every modern reader or viewer also knows in advance. What Sophocles dramatized was rather Oedipus's belated endeavor to discover who killed his royal predecessor and his slow realization that he himself was that most wanted killer—and that, into the bargain, his victim was his own father and his victim's widow, whom he had promptly taken to wife, his own mother. In other words, the action is not that of fate ensnaring Oedipus, but of Oedipus digging down into the dirty work that fate has already done. I use the term "fate" here playfully, without meaning to hypostatize it any more than Sophocles did. Through an ironic twist of fate, so to say, a befuddled Oedipus in Sophocles has tripped himself up in running the wrong way from a misleading prophecy that then wound up accidentally fulfilled. If the tale has a moral, that moral is: ignore oracles and they will pass you by. For its moral to have been instead that Oedipus's lot was divinely decreed as every son's "inescapable fate,"[1] that fate should at least have been foretold at Oedipus's birth. Then, however, the oracle prophesied only that Oedipus would kill his father[2] or, as the shepherd told to expose him recollects, his parents.[3] Indeed, his parricide was first off an exposed child's revenge, the very stuff of Greek creation myths from Uranus to Zeus. Not until he goes to Delphi as a grown-up does a second oracle there tack that second, marital clause onto the prophecy, and then with the rider that his mother would bear him children. Thus the prophecy binding on Oedipus from birth was only one term of the future "Oedipus complex" and not the other—the parricide without the incestuous payoff. Nor does Sophocles' Oedipus personify the wish, conscious or unconscious, to kill one's father and marry one's mother, for he has never loathed the father whom he kills or loved the mother whom he marries, having never known either of them before, and he goes to great lengths, albeit incautiously, to escape that dire double prospect. Finally, this stupendous tragedy by Sophocles appeals no less to women than to men, whereas Oedipus's lot was distinctly not a woman's. The importance, if not the all-importance, of what Freud called the Oedipus complex for human emotional development can be argued; its importance for the abiding appeal of Sophocles' masterpiece cannot.

On the other hand, an unrelated, gender-blind, universal psychic mechanism informing Sophocles' dramatization of the Oedipus legend may well contribute to whatever fascination it has exercised down the ages. I refer to the mechanism of traumatic reliving, which indeed, besides animating Sophocles' *Oedipus the King*, pervades much of the great literature of the West. This is the mechanism whereby we contrive unconsciously to relive our traumatic experiences in disguise, altering them in the process mainly in that we become their perpetrator in each case rather than their victim. The fictionist as a rule, above all the playwright, must make that disguise unnaturally thin in order for the reliving by the protagonist to come through as such to the reader or spectator, however dimly. In his *Oedipus the King*, Sophocles rendered that disguise well-nigh transparent.

Sophocles' play, be it remembered, begins with a plague on the city of Thebes that Apollo indicates he will lift only if King Laius's murderer of many years past is found out and punished. Laius's successor, Oedipus, promptly opens an investigation, only to discover before the day is done that he himself is that culprit whom he seeks. The facts that he turns up in the process are these. His father, who was Laius himself, pinned his feet together in his third day of life, and his mother, Queen Jocasta, gave him to a palace shepherd to expose on Mount Cithaeron, a passing oracle having predicted that a son to be born to the two of them would grow up to kill his father or (as stated once alternatively) his parents. The compassionate shepherd in turn gave baby Oedipus to a herdsman from Corinth who took him to the Corinthian king and queen. They, being childless, raised him as their own. In his young manhood Oedipus one day heard a drunk at a banquet cry out that he was not the king's son. Though his foster parents reassured him, he remained troubled enough to seek counsel at Delphi. There the oracle told him only (in this reverse order) that he would beget children with his mother and would kill his father. So he ran aimlessly, blindly, away from Corinth to escape that fate—and right smack up against a horse-drawn party that tried to push him off the road. Refusing to yield, he was struck over the head by the aging chief of the party, whom he instantly slew in a rage along with, as he thought, the whole escort, though in fact one witness escaped—the very slave who had given him away as a baby. For his victims were King Laius and a royal escort headed for Delphi, presumably to consult the oracle about the Sphinx then ravaging Thebes. Resuming his flight, Oedipus encountered this chimerical she-scourge head-on—a winged and claw-footed lioness with a woman's face and torso who devoured passersby outside the city one by one as they failed to solve her riddles. Oedipus, however, succeeded in solving the riddle she put to him, with the twofold result that she took her own life and jubilant Thebes acclaimed him as successor to Laius's throne and bed. He begot four children with Jocasta long before Apollo visited that new plague on the city for having left Laius's unidentified murderer at large after a brief inquest by Jocasta's brother, Creon, had foundered on the surviving witness's testimony that a whole band of thieves did Laius in.

All this background to the onstage action, this "preplay," emerges from the onstage proceedings themselves as Oedipus consults with the Priest, the Chorus, and Jocasta, questions the prophet Tiresias, interrogates Creon, cross-

examines the Corinthian herdsman of yore, shakes down the Theban ex-shep-
herd, and searches his own memory until the devastating truth is all too clear.
By then Jocasta has hanged herself. Following Jocasta into the palace, Oedipus
blinds himself with the pins from her robes, then returns to command and beg
Creon:

> Let me live on the mountains, on Cithaeron,
> my favorite haunt, I have made it famous.
> Mother and father marked out that rock
> to be my everlasting tomb—buried alive.
> Let me die there, where they tried to kill me.[4]

With this express wish to die on Mount Cithaeron, Oedipus closes out a
double cycle of traumatic reliving—two successive relivings, successively bigger
and better, of the trauma that dominated his life. This trauma is the one that he
suffered when, because of a prophecy, he was thrust from his home in Thebes
into exile before he was a full three days old. Some twenty years later he fled his
adoptive home in Corinth into exile in Thebes because of that same prophecy
somewhat elaborated. This was a classic reliving, with only the geographic
reversal to disguise it. Onstage, Oedipus relives the same trauma another
twenty-odd years later when he goes into exile yet again from his home in Thebes
because of that very same prophecy, now fulfilled. Closing out the cycle, he goes
(or, to be exact, asks to go) not all the way back to Corinth, but midway back
to the site of his traumatic "haunt," as he calls it,[5] on Mount Cithaeron.

Both Oedipus's trauma itself and its first reliving belong to the preplay of
Oedipus the King; its second reliving constitutes the play proper. Sophocles set
forth the mechanism of traumatic reliving with consummate skill not just for
that second bout of reliving, which unfolds onstage, but, through the preplay,
for the first reliving as well while even reaching back into the infantile trauma
itself for good measure. I say *through* the preplay because the inner experience
of the trauma as it was originally lived and relived is no part of the preplay
proper—no part of what the onstage action reveals outright about earlier events
informing it. In Sophocles' script the traumatic preplay shapes the play from
the start, and this ever more openly as the play advances. This is indeed the
very sense and substance of *Oedipus the King*: how what we have done, however
thoughtlessly, may come back with a vengeance to haunt what we do long
afterwards.[6]

But this Sophoclean preplay in turn has its subtext, by which I mean first
how the spectator or reader, sympathizing with the hero, must implicitly fill
in the blanks of that bare course of past events from the hero's vantage point.
Nor does only this preplay of Sophocles' *Oedipus the King* have such a subtext;

every preplay does. Take *Agamemnon* by Aeschylus, with which high tragedy began. At its outset Clytemnestra awaits the return from Troy of its conquering hero, Agamemnon, and the Chorus reminds us that on his way to Troy ten years earlier Agamemnon had sacrificed his daughter by Clytemnestra to favor his expedition. Even with this reminder slanted to regretful Agamemnon, we cannot help feeling Clytemnestra's old outrage still burning beneath her queenly demeanor. This outrage is one main clause of the subtext of Aeschylus's *Agamemnon*—of its oversized hero being cut down to size. In Sophocles' *Oedipus the King*, for its part, the subtext consists above all of Oedipus's own experience of his trauma and of its earlier reliving.

How then did Sophocles' Oedipus experience that trauma and its initial reliving before the play proper begins? First things first: the trauma was inflicted on Oedipus when, to start off his life, his father pinned his feet together and his mother gave him to be exposed. It is expressive of the lifelong impact of this trauma defining Oedipus's very identity for the Greeks that he was named for the conspicuous lesion it left, which stamped his body indelibly by the same token that it stamped his mind. For *oidipous* in ancient Greek meant, roughly, "swell-foot" or in effect "both feet swollen," the stigma or brandmark left by that painful pinning. Of course no one supposed that the infant retained a structured memory of the events of what in Sophocles' text is called his "worst hour,"7 but its impact would have been only the more profound—the imprint on the newborn babe's wholly tender, wholly vulnerable sensibility of an abrupt wrenching away from the snug comfort of his mother's body and a lacerating pinthrust through his ankles.

Sophocles conveyed this inward impress without outward memory ever so finely in a brief exchange between Oedipus and the former Corinthian herdsman. Oedipus asks in his haughtiest policeman's manner: "A herdsman, were you? A vagabond, scraping for wages?"8 To this provocation the old servant, now a messenger, replies gently and, for irony's sake, paternally: "Your savior too, my son, in your worst hour."9 Immediately Oedipus's tone changes at this kindly framing of a dire reminder. "When you picked me up," he asks, "was I in pain? What exactly?"10 He has all at once forgotten his criminal investigation even as he has snatched instead at the chance to fill in the gaping void at the pit of his memory. In the Greek original he even asks in the present progressive tense about having been picked up while in pain: this conveys the enduring immediacy of the experience ever so starkly. "Your ankles . . . ," the messenger replies, "they tell the story. Look at them."11 That is, they should long since have told him the story of his painful intended exposure. Oedipus, recoiling now, exclaims: "Why remind me of that, that old affliction?"12 Ignoring Oedipus's recoil, the messenger explains: "Your ankles were pinned together. I set you free"—this again in the present progressive tense: I *am setting you* free.[13] Oedipus, still flinching, demurs: "That dreadful mark—I've had it from the cradle."[14] Having just been told where the mark came from, which needed no telling at that, he acknowledges only that it went way back, like a birthmark. Ignoring this rejoinder in its turn, the Corinthian goes on: "And you got your name from that misfortune too, the name's still with you."[15]

This affirmation by the Corinthian messenger, that Oedipus was named for having had his feet pinned together as an infant slated for exposure, points to another capital fact about his earliest misadventure: that it was common knowledge in Corinth. Not just his name and his pierced ankles broadcast it about the land. The Corinthian herdsman who took the infant to his king and queen knew them to be childless against their will.[16] So too, assuredly, did all of Corinth. Nor can the queen very well have jumped the gun and simulated a pregnancy in anticipation of this "gift" of a child from the herdsman's hands[17] so as to fool the realm into thinking it was biologically hers while swearing the herdsman to silence. On the contrary, what that drunk blurted out at that banquet long years later, that Oedipus was not the king's own son, can have come as news to no one there except Oedipus himself. And this singularity in turn attests to the prodigious dodge by which Oedipus managed throughout his whole childhood and adolescence to fend off awareness of this open secret, this notorious basic fact about himself that spoke out of his very name and deformity. For anyone traumatized as was Oedipus, denial is the normal way of reacting before reenacting. The very concept of denial or evasion implies, of course, that the thing denied or evaded is known without being acknowledged, for it must be known in order to be sidestepped until—to return to Oedipus—a drunk shoves it right at one. Oedipus's strenuous early apprenticeship in denial, or evasion, of his conspicuous traumatic origins was to show in each of his two traumatic relivings. His deft self-training in not seeing the obvious can also be recognized as the source of his compensatory skill at reading riddles or solving mysteries.

If it was notorious in Corinth that Oedipus was a foundling, it was not likely a secret in Thebes either that the royal couple had disposed of their son. Jocasta's pregnancy must have been evident toward the last, and the newborn child was around for nearly three days before being given to a palace slave to expose. Even the oracle that preceded the child's birth would have been public; certainly the servant who bore the child away knew of that oracle, however inaccurately. To be sure, that tight-lipped Theban shepherd did not divulge the child's parentage, let alone the curse on its head, to his opposite number from Corinth; indeed, he could not do so lest the child be rejected. He was, though, known to be Laius's man.[18] Wind must soon enough have reached Corinth of the royal couple's disposal of their son because of that prophecy of parricide. Would Oedipus, then, have failed to put two and two together, if only under the sign of denial?

The prophecy of parricide surfaced beyond all possible denial in his traumatic complex when Oedipus consulted Apollo at Delphi about the drunk's disclosure, which was gnawing away at him. I say consulted Apollo about that disclosure because such is the force of his later, cagey onstage account of this trip to Delphi even with its claim that his foster parents had reassured him when he questioned them about his parenthood the day after that disclosure.[19] But if so, why had he gone to Delphi? He can say why no more clearly than that the god, when questioned, "denied the facts I came for."[20] At any rate, the drunk's disclosure, knocking the lid off Oedipus's traumatic complex, set the traumatic reliving in motion. Again he left his home and palace, whereupon he took his cue from the dire double prophecy that now confronted him and, rather than foil fate by returning to his adoptive parents, denied the evidence of his adoption all over again and rushed on heedlessly as if in a trance to kill a man old enough to be his father and marry a woman old enough to be his mother. Then he ended his homeless exile once more in a royal bedchamber, indeed right back at square one, having paused only for a prodigious stunt of puzzle solving along the way. Traumatic reliving is characterized by just such headlong, imperious urgency that overrides all obstacles, bends all alien wills, and twists fortune itself to its purpose. With Sophocles' Oedipus, this traumatic frenzy runs its course openly onstage only the second time around, when he re-relives. But Sophocles' subtext yields two fine examples of it even for his first spell of reliving.

The first example centers in the soft-hearted Theban royal slave who, rather than expose the accursed royal baby on Jocasta's orders, gave it to his Corinthian counterpart for adoption. Likeliest he did so with the childless Corinthian royal couple in mind. Certainly he knew his man thereafter in the swell-footed prince of Corinth, and just as certainly he recognized his man when, attached to Laius's party on that fatal excursion to Delphi, he alone escaped slaughter by irate Oedipus to return home to the palace in Thebes. Evidently he escaped unseen by Oedipus, who later assures Jocasta: "I killed them all—every mother's son!"[21] Subsequent testimony about the survivor's return to Thebes is divergent as to the time scheme. Creon recalls having questioned the terrified escapee while the Sphinx was still chanting and riddling,[22] whereas Jocasta recollects: "Soon as he returned from the scene and saw you on the throne with Laius dead and gone, he knelt and clutched my hand, pleading with me to send him into the hinterlands, to pasture, far as possible, out of sight of Thebes"[23]—which was, then, after the Sphinx's demise. Of the two, Jocasta's rather than Creon's would seem to be the confused memory, for her account leaves no time for Creon to have questioned the witness. Indeed, Jocasta leaves no time for Creon's investigation at all when she tells Oedipus: "The heralds no sooner reported Laius dead than you appeared and they hailed you King of Thebes."[24] On the other hand, Jocasta's recollection of the slave kneeling and clutching her hand leaves no doubt that he had recognized Laius's murderer in Oedipus on the throne just as some days earlier he had recognized Oedipus in Laius's murderer on the highway. Nor is the main point on which Jocasta and Creon, and indeed the Chorus, agree open to question: that the sole witness claimed that a whole band of thieves had attacked the Theban royal party.[25] Obviously that sole witness knew better, having lived through the event. By bearing false witness as he did, he put the truth under wraps for some twenty years. Conceivably he did so, once he saw the prophecy of parricide fulfilled, for fear lest his original failure to expose Oedipus be punished as a result. But he holds his tongue later even when Oedipus has offered "a handsome reward" for just such information as he tried so long to withhold.[26] When his tongue is finally loosened, moreover, no one moves to punish him despite his baleful perjury of twenty years' standing on top of his original transgression; indeed, by then his fateful tall tale about the band of thieves has been wholly forgotten even as his new deposition is taken unquestioningly at face value. Besides, such a personal precaution even on a slave's part should have been washed away in "a black sea of terror"[27] at the prospect of a father- and king-killer on the loose, then of his wedding his own mother and ruling the polis—though again, once all this was established fact, he might have thought that what the Thebans didn't know wouldn't hurt them. Earlier, while reeling away from the massacre, he can only have intended to cover up the parricide from Oedipus himself by fabricating that band of thieves. Yet he would not have felt for the raging killer any tender solicitude such as he had felt for the wounded baby under sentence of death. The long and short of these cross-indications is that, in Sophocles' scenario, this false witness to Oedipus's crime has all the look of someone simply swept along in someone else's prepotent pursuit of an imperative purpose. Such pursuits are trauma-driven.

The second person swept along against all reason by Oedipus on his first, frenzied stint of traumatic reliving was at the loftiest remove from that palace slave: Jocasta. The Delphic oracle had gone into one of Oedipus's ears and out the other, serving him only to duplicate a single element of the trauma behind his name: the original oracle, now enlarged. For the rest, on reaching Thebes he showed no more curiosity about the murdered king than about his own murder victims. Nor did he look behind the queen's twenty-year stretch of sterility that he now ended even as it had begun with his intended exposure.[28]

But Jocasta, for all the scorn she later professes for "the seers and their revelations,"[29] did believe in them enough to give her son by Laius ("my baby"[30]) to be killed because of a seer's prediction;[31] her counterassertion to Oedipus that it was Laius who gave the child to be killed can be discounted.[32] Still in all, ever so fast upon her husband's murder, which necessarily put her in mind of the old prophecy, she married a stranger from afar whose age would have been her exposed son's, indeed with ankle marks such as Laius's grim handiwork would have left. In one version of the Oedipus legend Jocasta recognizes Oedipus by those very ankle marks. Sophocles, however, even while highlighting the telltale deformity ("Your ankles . . . they tell the story," the Corinthian messenger says to Oedipus[33]), has Jocasta overlook it from her bridal chamber on out. It can hardly be supposed that Sophocles' Jocasta has been blinded by a hankering after incest, for she hangs herself when the truth comes home to her. Rather, she too has simply fallen in with Oedipus's compelling need to relive.

Oedipus's second bout of reliving runs its course onstage: it constitutes Sophocles' play proper. What sets it going, after another twenty-odd years of quietude, is the plague that befalls Thebes in punishment for having left Laius's murderer at large all that time. On the communal level the plague is a throwback to the Sphinx's visitation, another ghastly collective trauma that likewise began with a ruler's transgression and ended with a mystery solved. Why Apollo waited that long to chasten Thebes for letting Laius's murderer go unavenged while royal incest flourished there—Oedipus and Jocasta had borne and bred four children together—goes unexplained except insofar as the delay served Sophocles to point up the symmetry between Oedipus's first and second relivings after twenty-odd years each. Moreover, once the plague has supplied the equivalence with Oedipus's previous, Sphinx-jinxed round of reliving, it is lost from sight onstage as Oedipus, trauma-ridden, makes Apollo's injunction to Thebes to avenge Laius's murder his own and throws himself single-mindedly, tirelessly, relentlessly on the track of the murderer, oblivious of all else including Jocasta's welfare and his own.

In its frenetic pace and drastic literalness, this second reliving escalates the first. At the same time it repeats distinctive elements of that first reliving on top of the original trauma in its entirety. By way of repeating the earlier reliving, Oedipus above all solves a second riddle and thereby lifts a second death curse from Thebes, driving Jocasta, like the Sphinx before her, to suicide in the process. As for reliving the trauma now again, Oedipus winds up mutilated anew, having this time gouged out his two eyes, besides being torn away from his mother's body anew and prospectively exiled anew—such at least is his final request—to the spot on Mount Cithaeron where he had been intended to die in the first place. But this new maiming and new exposure also resonate with the previous reliving through an elided passage of the preplay familiar to all fifth-century Athenians. Blind Oedipus headed for exile at the close, "a stick tapping before him step by step," as the prophet Tiresias foretells it,[34] matches man's third age in the Sphinx's riddle that Oedipus solved about what creature walks first on four feet, then on two, and finally on three: such were indeed Oedipus's own three traumatic ages. Thus as a rule the onstage reliving simply conflates the original traumatic experience and its first reexperience, as when Sophocles contrived to work into his plot the news that the King of Corinth has died and Oedipus has been asked to succeed him: this summons to the royal palace in Corinth recalls the original traumatic sequence even while the summons to succeed a dead king recalls the first traumatic reliving. The Corinthian messenger's convenient appearance with that news at an opportune juncture of Oedipus's criminal investigation—for that messenger is none other than the shepherd who had taken baby Oedipus to the King of Corinth some forty years earlier—is, to be sure, an all-too-far-out instance of a traumatic reliving plying fate to its purposes. But it is just that far out in Sophocles' plot itself without seeming so.

I spoke of the "frenetic pace" of this second, onstage reliving: in just a few hours Oedipus gets to the bottom of a twenty-year-old crime with which Creon and all Thebes had got nowhere at the time. "We did our best, of course, discovered nothing," Creon recollects.[35] But this whirlwind drive by Oedipus to "bring it all to light myself," as he puts it,[36] is only half of a story of which his blindness to glaring facts is the paradoxical other half. Sophocles surpassed himself in dramatic skill—and that is saying something—in combining these two contradictory motifs: Oedipus the obtuse supersleuth following up every least clue with breathless dispatch even while being so ludicrously slow on the uptake. Straight off, Oedipus the top cop summons the blind seer Tiresias and provokes him into revealing his "dreadful secrets"[37]—the whole truth in a mantic nutshell—only to reject Tiresias's testimony out of hand in a rabid huff. Even Jocasta, mired in the same guilt trap as Oedipus, averse to the whole inquest, skeptical of all the evidence brought forth, catches on well before Oedipus although her counterargument of the "whole band" of thieves[38] goes uncontradicted to the last: screaming "Aieeeeee" to her "man of agony,"[39] she runs off and hangs herself while Oedipus, now at last inescapably aware that he had been brought to Corinth from Mount Cithaeron as a baby put out there to die, still muses about his uncertain parentage while awaiting the next witness to shake down.

That Oedipus at bottom all along knows just what he is struggling against himself to find out emerges even from a couple of masterstrokes of Sophocles' reed. In the beginning, after Apollo commands Thebes to "pay the killers back" for King Laius's murder,[40] Creon relates that the sole surviving witness could say clearly "just one thing": that "a whole band" of thieves and not a single hand "cut King Laius down."[41] Oedipus thereupon exclaims incongruously in the singular: "A thief, so daring, so wild, he'd kill a king? Impossible."[42] For good measure Oedipus corrects that eyewitness and Apollo once again the same way when he asks Creon a few lines later: "What stopped you from tracking down the killer then and there?"[43] He draws the implication himself in due course when he tells Jocasta after convoking the eyewitness: "If he refers to one man, one alone, clearly the scales come down on me."[44] In going such lengths to know and not to know, Oedipus repeats the scheme of his trip to Delphi to learn the very facts he was studiously looking away from. Likewise, his discovering his guilt even while evading it repeats the scheme of his running from Delphi right smack up against his fate even while fleeing it. Small wonder that in a final dodge he blames Apollo ("Apollo, friends, Apollo—he ordained my agonies!"[45]) even though Apollo was so far out of it that he too fell for the slave's false witness to a band of thieves ("Apollo commands us now—he could not be more clear, 'Pay the killers back' "[46]).

In brief, Sophocles' Oedipus lived out of a trauma incurred in the third day of his existence, reenacting it transparently at the two great junctures of his later life. Freud, who read his own father-and-mother complex into Sophocles' play, evidently did nonetheless dimly recognize Oedipus's constitutive trauma, for he simply displaced it from foot to penis in his model of the boyhood "Oedipus complex." Oedipus's constitutive trauma was, of course, at its physical core, the foot wound inflicted on Oedipus by his father with his mother's compliance. The complex that Freud named for Sophocles' Oedipus centered in the boy's wish to kill his father and marry his mother, as Sophocles' Oedipus did in fact do. But to this stock clause of his so-called Oedipus complex Freud added a stock climax: castration by the father, originally practiced, latterly only a threat often voiced by the mother in the father's name when it is not simply imagined by the child. In Freud's books, this traumatic threat was decisive for the subsequent life of the individual. It had no literal referent in Sophocles' play. But it did have a clear counterpart in Oedipus's traumatic foot maiming at his father's hands with his mother's compliance.[47]

I have saved the bottom line for the last. Oedipus's trauma of exposure twice relived in *Oedipus the King* was itself a traumatic reliving even if Oedipus himself did not contrive it. For that exposure reconfigured the primal, lacerating severance of birth, when (to quote another self-exiled tragic king) "the first time that we smell the air / We wawl and cry."[48] This universal referent for the trauma driving Oedipus is just what drives that trauma home subtextually to

Sophocles' public of all times and climes as Oedipus breaks open the old seals on his fate for a final, onstage reliving. His inner compulsion to relive is, on the surface, the outer compulsion of a sealed fate. These two compulsions are respectively the undertheme and overtheme of *Oedipus the King*. It is their dialectical interplay that makes even the foregone conclusion of *Oedipus the King* suspenseful.

Repetitions abound in Greek drama, mostly in the form of variations—this perhaps because that drama originated in music. The tragic playwrights drew largely on the same oft-told tales. Thus Sophocles' *Oedipus the King* adapted a familiar legend also dramatized by Aeschylus and Euripides in works now lost. Aeschylus's *Oresteia* grandly illustrates repetition in Greek plays other than Sophocles' *Oedipus the King*: witness Clytemnestra's triumphant display of her two slain victims, Agamemnon and his mistress Cassandra, at the close of *Agamemnon*, followed by Orestes' triumphant display of his two slain victims, Clytemnestra and her lover Aegisthus, at the close of *Choephoroe*. But of the surviving Greek tragedies only Sophocles' *Oedipus the King* dealt with traumatic reliving, which adds two things to mere repetition: one, trauma, and two, reliving.

Traumatic reliving has, however, figured as subtext in other literatures in the West, and most prominently in modern drama. A child's crippling through parental neglect is relived as that child's drowning through parental neglect in the powerful first act of Ibsen's *Little Eyolf*.[49] The subject of Pirandello's *Six Characters in Search of an Author* and his *Henry IV* is in each case transparently a trauma relived to a fatal outcome. And in Sartre's *No Exit* three damned souls each use the other two to relive their mortal traumas perpetually. As far as I can tell, though, the theme of traumatic reliving was unknown before Sophocles. It was not intrinsic to the Oedipus legend, which came in countless variants: Sophocles picked out just those that, taken together, described a pattern of traumatic reliving. He even threw in a few of his own devising for good measure, such as Oedipus's concluding wish to be put out to die right where his parents had originally put him out to die on Mount Cithaeron; once it served to nail down the reliving in *Oedipus the King*, this last wish was duly forgotten by the time of Sophocles' later *Oedipus at Colonus*, which is all about where Oedipus will die. So too was traumatic reliving itself left behind in old Greece after *Oedipus the King* as far as the records disclose. By all indications it was a one-shot dramatic device of a tragedian who appears to have renewed himself continually. As with so much from Sophocles, that one shot was right on target not just dramatically, but (pace Freud) psychoanalytically as well.

NOTES

1. Sigmund Freud, *Gesammelte Werke*, vol. 11 (London: Imago, 1940), 210.
2. Sophocles, *Oedipus the King*, in *The Three Theban Plays*, trans. Robert Fagles (New York: Penguin, 1984), 784–88.
3. Ibid., 1299.
4. Ibid., 1589–93.
5. Ibid., 1590.
6. This dominion of the preplay over the play in *Oedipus the King* makes a mockery of Aristotle's prescription in *The Poetics* that a tragedy should follow in its entirety from an absolute beginning on stage—and at that, Aristotle took Sophocles' *Oedipus the King* to be the model tragedy.
7. Sophocles, *Oedipus the King*, 1129.
8. Ibid.
9. Ibid., 1129. The messenger's word for son or child, *téknon*, is even more maternal than paternal.
10. Ibid., 1130.
11. Ibid., 1131.
12. Ibid., 1132.
13. Ibid., 1133.
14. Ibid., 1134.
15. Ibid., 1135–36.
16. Ibid., 1122–23.
17. Ibid., 1117.
18. Ibid., 1143–46.
19. Ibid., 865 ("I was satisfied"—but *térpomai* in Sophocles' Greek is more like "gratified" or even "delighted").
20. Ibid., 870.
21. Ibid., 898.
22. Ibid., 133–49.
23. Ibid., 834–38.
24. Ibid., 812–13.
25. Ibid., 138–39; 788–90, 831–32, 938–40; 331.
26. Ibid., 262–65.
27. Ibid., 1682.
28. This suggests that Jocasta recognized Oedipus at least unconsciously; cf. later in this paragraph on his ankle marks. Euripides' *Ion* is comparable on a mother's sterility from infanticide.
29. Sophocles, *Oedipus the King*, 979.
30. Ibid., 794.
31. Ibid., 1289–99.
32. Ibid., 791–92.
33. Ibid., 1131.
34. Ibid., 519.

35. Ibid., 633.

36. Ibid., 150.

37. Ibid., 374.

38. Ibid., 931–42.

39. Ibid., 1176.

40. Ibid., 122.

41. Ibid., 136, 139–40.

42. Ibid., 139–41.

43. Ibid., 146–47.

44. Ibid., 935–37.

45. Ibid., 1467–68.

46. Ibid., 120–22 (emphasis added).

47. James Murphy suggests that Freud's replacement of foot piercing by castration may have been mediated by baby Freud's circumcision at roughly Oedipus's traumatic age (private communication).

48. William Shakespeare, *King Lear*, IV.vi.177–78. Cf. Sophocles, *Oedipus at Colonus*, in *The Three Theban Plays*, trans. Robert Fagles (New York: Penguin, 1984), 1388–91: "Not to be born is best / when all is reckoned in, but once a man has seen the light / the next best thing, by far, is to go back / back where he came from, quickly as he can"—lines creepily appropriate to Oedipus's birth and first reliving.

49. In that same first act of *Little Eyolf* the mother exposes the mechanism of traumatic reliving in an exchange with the father just before the tragic climax. If little Eyolf has taken him away from her, she declares, she will throw herself into the arms of the first man who comes along, such as a road-builder who has just called on them. Then she's only joking, he replies, since that road-builder is attached to someone else. All the better, she exclaims, for then she would be doing to that someone else just what little Eyolf had done to her.

3

Blood for Blood
The Gospel According to Matthew

My next text is an extra-short one: the tale of the massacre of the innocents as it appears in the single document that reports it, the Gospel of Matthew. Here, for convenience, is the relevant passage from Matthew in full:

Now when Jesus was born in Bethlehem of Judea in the days of Herod the king, behold, wise men from the East came to Jerusalem, saying, "Where is he who has been born king of the Jews? For we have seen his star in the East, and have come to worship him." When Herod the king heard this, he was troubled, and all Jerusalem with him; and assembling all the chief priests and scribes of the people, he inquired of them where the Christ was to be born. They told him, "In Bethlehem of Judea; for so it is written by the prophet:

'And you, O Bethlehem, in the land of Judah,
are by no means least among the rulers of Judah;
for from you shall come a ruler
who will govern my people Israel.' "

Then Herod summoned the wise men secretly and ascertained from them what time the star appeared; and he sent them to Bethlehem, saying, "Go and search diligently for the child, and when you have found him bring me word, that I too may come and worship him." When they had heard the king they went their way; and lo, the star which they had seen in the East went before them, till it came to rest over the place where the child was. When they saw the star, they rejoiced exceedingly with great joy; and going into the house they saw the child with Mary his mother, and they fell down and worshiped him. Then, opening their treasures, they offered him gifts, gold and frankincense and myrrh. And being warned in a dream not to return to Herod, they departed to their own country by another way.

Now when they had departed, behold, an angel of the Lord appeared to Joseph in a dream and said, "Rise, take the child and his mother, and flee to Egypt, and remain there till I tell you; for Herod is about to search for the child, to destroy him." And he rose and took the child and his mother by night, and departed to Egypt, and remained there until the death of Herod. This was to fulfil what the Lord had spoken by the prophet, "Out of Egypt have I called my son."

Then Herod, when he saw that he had been tricked by the wise men, was in a furious rage, and he sent and killed all the male children in Bethlehem and in all that region who were two years old or under, according to the time which he had ascertained from the wise men. Then was fulfilled what was spoken by the prophet Jeremiah:

> "A voice was heard in Ramah,
> wailing and loud lamentation,
> Rachel weeping for her children;
> she refused to be consoled,
> because they were no more."[1]

The Gospel of Matthew, which contains this passage, was evidently written or compiled late in the first century of our era—too late for Jesus' disciple Matthew to have been its author, though it may have drawn on records kept by him.[2] It largely repeats the one Gospel produced earlier: that of Mark, which was published toward 70 A.D. But it reworks the material taken from Mark by way of stressing the messiahship of Jesus for Jewish readers. Its author or authors evidently also knew the still earlier writings by the apostle Paul, who spread to the Gentiles a message of salvation through faith in Jesus. Paul expressed a key tenet of this message when he affirmed of Jesus: "In him we have redemption through his blood."[3] This central tenet of Paul's message presumably prompted a remark ascribed by Matthew's Gospel to Jesus at the Last Supper: that his blood was to be "shed for many for the forgiveness of sins."[4] Conversely, whereas Paul compared attaining justification through faith, hope, and love to outgrowing childhood,[5] Matthew, following Mark's lead,[6] had Jesus declare instead to his disciples: "Unless you turn, and become as little children, you will never enter into the kingdom of heaven."[7]

These two themes of Matthew's taken from Paul and Mark respectively—that Jesus shed his blood to save others, and that salvation was for the likes of children exclusively—are crucial to the subtext of Matthew's tale of a massacre of the innocents, as will be seen. But that tale itself was not derivative, being nowhere on record in the first century outside of the Gospel of Matthew itself. Even Josephus's Jewish chronicles of roughly the same date are silent about any such gory outrage for all their insistent recounting of Herod's misdeeds. Thus the tale would seem to lack any and all foundation in fact. On the other hand, as Matthew's text was addressed to a Jewish readership living around the site of the putative event less than a century after its alleged occurrence, such a myth just may have been no ad hoc fabrication by Matthew but could have already arisen independently of him on the grounds of Herod's notorious cruelty together with his political insecurity as king of the Jews solely by the grace of Rome.

Literarily, the arresting Gospel narrative of the wise men's visit followed by the massacre and the flight into Egypt is all of a piece, unlike the patchwork effect of Matthew as a whole and even more so of the Bible overall. That brief narrative sequence accords with the main thrust of Matthew's Gospel in being designed to help show that Jesus was the long-awaited Messiah heralded by the prophets of old. A star signals to the wise men in the East the coming birth of the Christ. The same star reappears and guides them to Jesus' birthplace in the very town predesignated by the Scriptures. Heaven thereupon acts through two premonitory dreams, one sent down to those wise men and one to Joseph, which together serve to protect the newborn child from Herod's wrath. But most compellingly, every male child of Bethlehem young enough to be the Messiah by Herod's calculations perishes by Herod's orders except his intended victim, Jesus himself, whose narrow escape reveals him unmistakably as a favored child of heaven.

In sum, the force of baby Jesus' escaping that mythic massacre in Matthew was to help establish his messianic credentials. Well might a sophisticated Greco-Roman Jew reading Matthew have shrugged off the star and the dreams. But for Jesus alone to have survived a slaughter aimed at him alone spoke strongly for his divinity, or at all odds for his supernatural protection. Precedents in this same line of privileged biblical survivors of massive destruction went back to righteous Noah and his family, followed a few generations later by less righteous Lot and his two daughters. In Egypt afterwards Pharaoh has every son born to his Hebrew subjects cast into the Nile, but Pharaoh's daughter spots baby Moses hidden in the reeds—"and he became her son"[8] before being called to deliver his people. To cite just one further, literally glaring biblical example, when Elijah laments to the Lord that "the people of Israel have . . . slain thy prophets with the sword, and I, even I only, am left,"[9] the Lord has Elijah go on battling the rival prophets of Baal single-handedly pending his conveyance to heaven "in a chariot of fire."[10] Nor did the pagans then view survivorship any differently. Homer's Odysseus sees his companions all perish in a deadly shipwreck that he survives alone for a triumphant homecoming to Ithaca under the aegis of the goddess Athena. Only a century older than Matthew's Jesus in point of authorship was Virgil's pious warrior hero, Aeneas, whose mother, divine Venus, sees him safely through the defeat of his native Troy and, soon afterwards, a fierce storm at sea that ravages his fleet and following.[11] Consistently for Jew and Gentile alike, special dispensation from catastrophe bore on the very face of it the mark of a holy favor.

This tradition of blessed survival clinches it: Herod's massacre of the innocents was a fearful contrivance, or appropriation from legend, by the evangelist Matthew to drive home his sectarian point of Jesus' messiahship. Indeed, Matthew's messianic construction on that bloody business is the sum total of his commentary on it. In particular, his account evokes the shock and grief of the bereaved mothers in Bethlehem only indirectly, by dragging in Jeremiah on Rachel weeping in nearby Ramah for her children deported to Babylon (an exegetical sleight of hand, for the Lord assured Rachel: "Your children shall come back"[12]). And it cites those touching verses by Jeremiah only to claim this additional, strained prefiguration of the life of Jesus. Quite possibly it was that passage of Jeremiah which, together with Matthew's aim of showing prophecies fulfilled through the life of Jesus, inspired in Matthew that yarn of the massacre in the first place and, along with it, that matching tall tale of a flight into Egypt. Herod's innocent little victims themselves are faceless in Matthew's narrative, and God's failure to intervene on their behalf is absolutely no issue for Matthew. Even the pat term "massacre of the innocents" is not Matthew's; it first arose in a later age along with all of the compassion and indignation that it implies.

Thus on the textual level—to repeat this key indication both for clarity and for stress—the mythic massacre of the innocents was of no concern to Matthew, let alone to his Jesus, beyond its evidentiary value at that juncture of Matthew's special pleading for Jesus' messiahship. Matthew's subtext, however, turns that biblical scroll inside out as it tells an inner story of infinite remorse over that selfsame massacre. This divergent subtextual story can be approached partway under felicitous modern guidance: through a passage of *The Fall* by Albert Camus. The narrator of this inspired novel by Camus styles himself Jean-Baptiste Clamence and monologues throughout to a nameless, ensnared listener about his lapse from Edenic bliss into guilt unending. Once he asks rhetorically in passing: "Say, do you know why he was crucified?" only to provide his own answer: "The real reason is that he knew he wasn't quite innocent. . . . He must have heard about a certain massacre of the innocents—the children of Judea slaughtered while his parents carried him off to safety. Why did they die if not because of him? Those bloody soldiers, those children cut in two, filled him with horror. Yet, the way he was, I'm sure he couldn't forget them. And that sadness to be divined in all of his acts: wasn't it the incurable sorrow of one who, night after night, heard the voice of Rachel groaning over her little ones and refusing to be consoled?"[13] Camus's latter-day John the Baptist, having out-Matthewed Matthew here by conflating the bereaved mothers of Judea with their prefiguration in Rachel,[14] tops off his affecting account of Jesus' course to Calvary: "Knowing what he knew, aware of everything human—ah, who would have thought that it were less of a crime to cause death than not to die oneself!—faced day and night with his innocent crime, he found it too hard to bear up and keep going."[15]

This arresting surmise of a fatal survivor guilt in the scriptural Jesus due to his "innocent crime" is at odds with the manifest aim of Matthew's presentation, which was to add that miraculous survival to Christ's other marks of messianic identity. More, the survivor guilt surmised by Camus's fallen hero is just that much at variance with the whole heroic ethos of the ancient world as well. The ancients knew guilt for misdeeds, period. Not guiltily but "in hot anger"[16] does Moses, sometime escapee of Pharaoh's massacre of the newborn sons of Israel, turn the tablets on Pharaoh so that all the firstborn of Egypt die while only the Israelites are passed over. Across the Mediterranean, guilt pursues Orestes the mother murderer, not Odysseus the seasoned survivor, for all Odysseus's mourning of dead heroes. Nor did survivor guilt sound in Pericles' noble oration over the dead warriors of Athens—for theirs was "the best death"[17]—as it did in a comparable modern context through Lincoln's resounding resolve at Gettysburg "that these dead shall not have died in vain." Shame was another matter, as with Oedipus shamed before Thebes. Shame readily attached in antiquity to escaping that "best death," or surviving a defeat on the field, as when, by Herodotus's account, three hundred choice Spartan soldiers once lost a showdown battle against an even match of Argives: "It is said that Othryades, the sole survivor of the three hundred, was ashamed to return to Sparta after the death of his companions, and killed himself."[18] But the gods could shoo such soldierly shame away. Shamelessly Virgil's legendary warrior Aeneas flees his fallen city, glory-bound, at the behest of Venus, leaving the bereaved and victimized Trojan women behind for Euripides to memorialize. Lest Aeneas even pause to mourn his wife, lost in the shuffle, her ghost prevails upon him to go on alone.[19] His nugatory shame sounds faintly afterwards when he groans in the thick of his deadly storm at sea that he would sooner have gone down fighting for his native Troy.[20] No guilt, though, inheres in this noble leeward regret, which promptly evaporates anyway in his divine mother's snug protection. As for fair Helen, whose abduction it was that brought the dire carnage to Troy in the first place, she of all people should have felt guilt in the aftermath of the siege. Homer, though, allows her none despite the hint he once drops that she may have connived at her own misadventure, and Euripides, who blames her outright, has her blithely shift that blame to the gods when confronted by her conquering husband amid the ruins of the captive city.[21]

A basic distinction is overdue. Three of these comparable classic cases—Helen in Troy, Aeneas at sea, and Jesus in Bethlehem—involve a crucial factor lacking in simple survivor guilt of the sort rampant in our modern world. No mere survivors, these three ancients in these three instances were responsible, however unintentionally, for the calamities that they survived, whereas guilt plagues today's survivors of wars and other high-toll horrors that are in no way due to them personally. Thus in World War II it was a truism that "the fighters who get away with it feel guilty toward those who don't."[22] Likewise, few if any Jewish survivors of the Holocaust have endured their survival easily. Could it be credited, Jesus' survivor guilt à la Camus would, then, represent the first step of a two-step departure from ancient heroic to modern guilty survival. That is, the guilt felt by Matthew's Jesus for surviving a disaster due to him would lead to the guilt felt in modern times for simply surviving where others perish. Or rather, the guilt *mostly* felt nowadays: vestiges of the ancient heroic mode of blithe survival are still in evidence way down the scale of modern myths, as when the cop or soldier most in sympathy survives a gory cinematic shootout alone for a happy ending.

But can Camus's subtextual reading of Matthew be credited? It can—and, to begin with, on the ground of its intrinsic plausibility once that horrendous massacre decreed on Jesus' account is considered from Jesus' own vantage point, which Matthew's text ignores.[23] Even a consciousness formed in the ancient world, above all one informed by a heart as commiserate as that of Jesus, could not fail to feel some rudiments of guilt for such a lacerating, humanly irredeemable "innocent crime" that was its very birthmark. But that guilt beyond human redemption is only one of the three components of Matthew's subtext.

Its other two components inform the two themes cited at the outset: that heaven belongs to children, and that Jesus shed his blood to save others. Subtextually, Matthew's tale of the massacre of the innocents, taken together with these two themes, supplies the personal meaning for Jesus of redemption through his blood. At this subtextual level, whereas the child Jesus was saved while other children died on his account, the grown-up Jesus died to save others after first equating these others with children. Let me reconstruct this subtext in sequence so as to draw out its compact meaning. Paul's Jesus had spilled his life's blood that others might be saved. Mark's Jesus in turn had identified these others with children. Then Matthew tied these two strands of the Jesus story together subtextually with a band cut out of whole cloth as if for that very purpose: a children's massacre in Bethlehem that was meant for Jesus but that Jesus alone survived. Oddly, the cruel myth of the massacre of the innocents humanized the Redeemer's story on this subtextual level.[24] Matthew's subtextual Jesus did penance in kind for his unwitting, unwilling role in that ghastly massacre: blood for blood, saving for saving, with the humanly irredeemable divinely redeemed. He shed less blood than the innocents, to be sure, but he far outrescued his own solitary rescue from Herod. For he died to save us all and to save us eternally, whereas earlier he alone had been saved and in this world alone. The ledgers were infinitely overbalanced.

Though unhistorical, Herod's massacre of the baby boys of Bethlehem is not fictitious in the way of Oedipus's exposure and later self-exposure. For it was meant to be, and presumably was, seen as literal fact from the very first even by the descendants of those inhabitants of Bethlehem whose children aged two and under had not been slaughtered. Its credibility within the Matthew Gospel was nonetheless of the same order as that of the Oedipus legend dramatized by Sophocles insofar as it too depended on the tight fit between text and subtext. Sophocles' text and subtext both turn on fatedness, oracular and traumatic respectively; Matthew's both turn on vindication, with prophecy fulfilled on the textual and suffering redeemed on the subtextual plane. Sophocles' and Matthew's subtexts are as one, moreover, in treating a tragic destiny as a delayed reaction to a tragic sendoff in life.

The tight fit between Matthew's text and subtext was, then, one of symmetry or, perhaps better, of counterpoise. But did his text and subtext interact? The theme of Matthew's text is that Jesus was the Messiah, protected by heaven and prefigured by the holy prophecies. Matthew's subtext supplies a human, all-too-human reason for Jesus to have died that others might be saved. The single episode of the massacre of the innocents did not suffice for Matthew to make his textual case; he needed his other evidence of Jesus' messiahship as well. So did his subtext require, over and beyond that single episode, Jesus' identification of the justified with children and his talk of spilling his blood for others. But neither in calling the justified childlike nor in announcing his blood sacrifice does Matthew's Jesus fulfill a prophecy or enjoy divine protection. Only in that episode of the massacre do Matthew's overtheme and undertheme intersect. Or rather, they play off each other contrapuntally at that point, like themes in a fugue, the one otherworldly and the other worldly, the one transcendent and the other immanent, the one divine and the other human. They harmonize as they do because the redemptive subtext has the same circular form as the textual pattern of prophecy and fulfillment: Jesus comes full circle, as in a prophecy fulfilled, when he relives in reverse his experience of surviving the children's death on his account—that is, when he dies so that grown-up children might be saved. It goes with this formal overlap between text and subtext that time is collapsed in each of them and hence in both together. Even as prophecy and fulfillment converge in the timelessness of the divine perspective, so do the massacre and its redemption connect only in the timelessness of unconscious understanding, for neither Matthew nor his Jesus draws this connection between the massacre and its redemption any more consciously than do Matthew's readers. That is, Matthew's Jesus may be "faced day and night with his innocent crime," as Camus held, but he is no more aware that he is reliving it in reverse through his crucifixion than Sophocles' Oedipus is aware that he is reliving an exposure trauma or, just ahead, Thomas's and Gottfried's Tristan is aware that he is reliving a parental trauma.

Matthew's scriptural separation of the divine from the human as between the text and the subtext of this bloody episode of the massacre of the innocents did not carry over into Christian art. On the contrary, the iconography of the massacre increasingly highlighted the bereaved mothers' anguish, with Jesus' miraculous escape implicit, or sometimes even showing, behind the scenes. This elevation of the pathos in Matthew's subtext to pictorial text only underscores by contrast the radical separation of text from subtext in Matthew's Gospel itself despite their formal overlap there—the drastic dichotomy of divine and human that indeed characterized Christianity as a whole at its inception but could not be sustained beyond the historic first flush of the faith. On a Christian reading, the massacre prefigured the crucifixion, which in turn fulfilled Herod's purpose behind the massacre. Popular piety ratified this figural connection in setting the slaughtered babes, or holy innocents, beside the crucified Christ as the first martyrs to the faith and even saluting them from his heart, so to speak, as "the first victims of Christ."[25] Christian art later ratified this ratification. The massacred innocents, holding their martyrs' palms, entered into depictions of the Madonna and Child as a premonitory presence.[26] Barna da Siena put the massacre on top of the crucifixion in a painting of about 1355 for the Collegiata of San Gimignano, this juxtaposition being self-explanatory to Sienese worshippers.[27] The one moment interpenetrates the other here as, directly under the heap of babies already martyred, their winged souls circle a Christ on the cross being lanced the very way that the last little victim above him is still being lanced. To sharpen Barna's point, in his iconography those corpses over Christ's head are on Christ's mind. Nor was that all. A stock twosome of Tuscan renditions of the massacre from the 1260s on steals the sad scene in Barna: a bereaved mother isolated in her grief who holds her dead child diagonally across her lap.[28] This group of two was closely matched in Franciscan and Dominican statuary along the Rhine beginning around 1300 by a bereaved Mary deep in solitude who holds the dead Christ diagonally across her lap. The Tuscan mother lamenting a single child at once present and dead cannot have referred to Rachel weeping for her children alive and absent as in Matthew's quotation from Jeremiah[29]; the clearer indication is that she prefigured a solitary Mary alone with the dead Christ even before the Rhenish pietà emerged. Given its pronouncedly humanizing drift, all this visual linkage of Herod's massacre with Christ's death in the mode of figure and fulfillment, as in Matthew's text, argues their concurrent unconscious popular linkage in the mode of guilt and atonement, as in Matthew's subtext.

To return in conclusion to a theme left dangling earlier: survivor guilt has come a long way since its beginnings in Matthew's subtext. That long way is the more difficult to retrace since such guilt did not find outright expression before our own century as far as the historic records disclose. However clearly it sounded through Lincoln's Gettysburg Address, to recur to that example, it was still inexplicit even there. But the willing Christian martyr of old evidently already felt it toward other Christians massacred not on his or her account (unlike Matthew's innocents massacred on Jesus' account), but merely for being Christian: thence the martyrdom craze in the early Christian era. Christian survivor guilt could rise to fever pitch and still not emerge into the open: witness the flagellants proliferating among the survivors of the Black Death. Even uncrazed Christians in premodern Europe ought logically to have felt it in some measure if they merely survived childhood with its traumatic death rates. But as far as meets the historian's eye, Christian and then post-Christian survivor guilt has developed on the massacre model only, and in this it still bears the stamp of its origin in Matthew's Gospel. Similarly, its extension from the "innocent crime" of Matthew's Jesus to encompass survival pure and simple, with no felt responsibility for the slaughter survived, also bears an Israelitic stamp of origin insofar as, in their constitutive self-conception, "all Jews anywhere and anytime are inherently survivors" who "must atone for having been spared."[30]

Why did Christian survivor guilt remain unconscious as long as it did? A rich source for part of the answer is Petrarch's copious correspondence. In the course of his threescore years and ten Petrarch and his friends lost countless loved ones, so that his letters were rife with mourning and condoling. He came closest to expressing survivor guilt outright in 1362 following the death from the plague of both his dearest friend, nicknamed Socrates, and his wayward son, Giovanni. "I have no weightier grievance against my fortune," he wrote, "than that I, harder than a diamond, slower than a tortoise, and more lasting than a phoenix, have been kept waiting until now, while my friends were carried off before their time."[31] But, weighty as was his grievance against fate because of his own privileged survival, Petrarch insisted ever and again that every death, however untimely it might seem, was God's will and hence, as the start of life eternal, necessarily a blessing. Clearly, survivor guilt was inconsistent with this Christian sense of death as a blessing. That is one reason why it could lead only an underground existence in Christendom until the Christian afterlife lost its hold over the minds and hearts of believers and nonbelievers alike. Only with the Gospels desacralized did this legacy of Matthew's Jesus come out into the open. Then it came out in full force, and its full force is still rising.

But the decisive reason for its long latency turned on the centrality of the Passion to Christian piety. Where Greeks empathized with their tragic heroes for the length of a play, pious Christians empathized with the suffering Christ all their lives long. Only through such empathy could they pick up on the survivor guilt latent in Matthew's Gospel. Its very latency at the source then tended to keep survivor guilt under wraps. In this too the unwritten was a match for the written word.

NOTES

1. Matthew 2:1–18, as in *The Holy Bible*, Revised Standard Version, ed. Herbert G. May and Bruce M. Metzger (New York: Oxford University Press, 1971).

2. On the authorship and historicity of Matthew's Gospel, see especially Robin Lane Fox, *The Unauthorized Version: Truth and Fiction in the Bible* (New York: Knopf, 1992), 126–29 and passim; on this passage specifically, see also Raymond E. Brown, *The Birth of the Messiah: A Commentary on the Infancy Narratives in Matthew and Luke* (Garden City, NY: Doubleday, 1977), 226–28 and passim.

3. Ephesians 1:7; cf. Hebrews 13:12—and bloodlessly, 2 Corinthians 5:15, Galatians 1:3–4 and 4:5, 1 Thessalonians 5:9–10, Timothy 2:5–6, Titus 2:13–14, and Hebrews 2:9 and 9:28.

4. Matthew 26:28.

5. 1 Corinthians 13:9–11.

6. Mark 9:37, 10:14–15; further, Luke 18:15–17.

7. Matthew 18:3.

8. Exodus 2:10.

9. 1 Kings 19:14—but cf. 1 Kings 18:4.

10. 2 Kings 2:11.

11. Virgil, *Aeneid*, I:95–102, II:619–21; on Jupiter's extra protection, II:680–705.

12. Jeremiah 31:16.

13. Albert Camus, *Théâtre, récits, nouvelles* (Paris: Pléiade, 1962), 1530–31.

14. Ibid., 1531: "The plaint arose in the night, Rachel called to her children killed for him, and he was alive!"

15. Ibid.

16. Exodus 11:8.

17. Thucydides, *The History of the Peloponnesian War*, II:44.

18. Herodotus, *The Histories*, trans. Aubrey de Sélincourt (London: Penguin, 1972), 74.

19. Virgil, II:738–89.

20. Ibid., I:94–101.

21. Euripides, *The Trojan Women*, 914–65.

22. Arthur Koestler, *Arrival and Departure* (London: Jonathan Cape, 1943), 160; cf. Brett Kahr, *D. W. Winnicott: A Biographical Portrait* (London: Karnac, 1996), 115.

23. In the twelfth century, when Jesus' humanity was stressed, an ivory altarpiece showed him watching the massacre in shock and horror from his mother's arms (Salerno cathedral museum); an early-thirteenth-century miniature showed him pointing to it from the same snug spot, only deadpan (Paris, Bibliothèque Nationale, lat. 11560, fol. 86r).

24. Subtextually Matthew's Jesus is *too* human in that his felt guilt accorded ill with his sinlessness. Perhaps this felt guilt is why he took baptism on his return to Israel after Herod's death: Matthew 3:13–17.

25. Prudentius, *Hymn to the Innocents*, 2: "Vos prima Christi victima."

26. James Hall, *Dictionary of Subjects and Symbols in Art* (London: John Murray, 1974), 205.

27. Already on Giovanni Pisano's Pistoia pulpit of 1301 (Sant'Andrea) the massacre of the innocents is directly left of the crucifixion.

28. For such lap-type pietà-like figures in Tuscan and Umbrian massacre scenes of the time, see Nicola Pisano (Siena, Duomo: 1266–1268); *Antiphonarium nocturnum* (Siena, Museo dell'Opera del Duomo, Corale 33–5: c. 1290); *Supplicationes variae* (Florence, Laurenziana, Plut 25.3, fol. 368v: toward 1300); Giotto (Assisi, Lower Church of San Francesco: toward 1300); Perugian miniaturist (Perugia, Biblioteca Capitolare, ms. 9, c. 100v: toward 1300); School of Giotto (Assisi, Basilica di Santa Chiara: toward 1300); Giovanni Pisano (Pistoia, Duomo: 1301, and Pisa, Duomo: 1302–1311); Duccio di Buoninsegna (Siena, Museo dell'Opera del Duomo: 1308–1311). The prototype for this group can be traced as far back as the Sacramentary of Drogo (Paris, Bibliothèque Nationale, lat. 9428, fol. 31a: c. 850).

29. Cf. Hall, 205. A likelier Rachel figure in Tuscan massacres is an occasional wailing mother *not* holding a child.

30. Howard F. Stein, "Judaism and the Group-Fantasy of Martyrdom," *Journal of Psychohistory*, 6 (1978): 166, 186.

31. Francis Petrarch, *Letters of Old Age*, trans. Aldo S. Bernardo, Saul Levin, and Reta A. Bernardo (Baltimore: Johns Hopkins University Press, 1992), I, 8.

4

In You My Death, in You My Life
The Tristan Legend

If, as Freud held, the Oedipus legend presents a universal childhood wish as fulfilled, it disguises that fulfillment beyond recognition by postponing it to adulthood and positing it as a trick of fate. But the complex that Freud named after Oedipus informs another, later legend with telltale childlike naïveté through all its tellings and retellings, however sophisticated: the Tristan legend. Young Tristan acts out that Freudian complex not with real parents unrecognized, as does Oedipus, but with patent parental proxies, which makes at least as much Freudian sense. Starkly Freudian besides is Tristan's penalty of a deadly sex wound as compared with Oedipus's self-blinding and banishment in Sophocles' script.

Suppose that before Sophocles took it up, the Oedipus legend did tacitly convey the Freudian baby boy's fantasy of killing his father and marrying his mother: if so, Sophocles tacitly overwrote a childhood wish fulfilled with a perinatal trauma relived. This, oddly, is just what two medieval master metrists known only by name, Thomas of Britain and Gottfried von Strassburg, did when they blended a received Freudian-style subtext into a second, quasi-Sophoclean one of Thomas's devising to give the Tristan legend its supreme formulation. Tristan indulges a Freudian father-and-mother complex in both poets' rhymed romances—a French epic of about 1160 by Thomas, recast in German by Gottfried a half century later—as flagrantly as in rival Tristan sagas, and then some. But in theirs he does so only incidentally to reliving, like Sophocles' Oedipus and indeed Matthew's Jesus, an existential trauma at the very source and core of his being.

Myths are childish. In reworking them, a sophisticated poet will rationalize away or gloss over their most naïvely magical elements. Some hard-core prodigies will remain untouchable, to be sure—a riddling sphinx here, a fire-breathing dragon there. But Thomas and then Gottfried did play down or spoof up the simplistically fabulous stuff that still looms so large in other Tristan romances of their time. Chief among such rival, older-style Tristans were Béroul's in French and Eilhart von Oberge's in German, both of about 1190 and both based on a still more primitive written source,[1] itself presumably derived, at some remove, from oral tradition. The numerous extant medieval variants of the legend, from the Celtic to the Byelorussian, cannot be reduced with any certainty to a common original. Nonetheless some characters, episodes, and motifs ran through them all to constitute a common European heritage. Ironically, the tale they tell is, in its subtext, as unequivocally Oedipal in the Freudian sense as Sophocles' *Oedipus the King*, the Freudian locus classicus, is not.

The Freudian father-and-mother complex is conspicuous already in Tristan's earliest Celtic exploits and intrigues. Of these rudiments of Tristan's later legend,[2] the two core morsels date back to the ninth century or even before. In one, an Irish chieftain's young wife and his trusted nephew, enchanted by a magic spell, run off together. In the other, a hero slays a dragon to deliver a princess, then foils false claimants to the deed and to her hand as she heals his wound from the combat.

In time that Irish chieftain from the one primal strand of the legend evolved into King Mark of England, his bride into Princess Isolde of Ireland, and the magic spell into a love potion meant for their nuptials but mistakenly drunk by Isolde together with Mark's trusted nephew escorting her from Dublin: Tristan.[3] An illicit amour ensues, passionate and painful. On its flip side it is a classic Freudian family romance down to its fated, fatal finale. In it Mark, as Tristan's maternal uncle, fronts for Tristan's father. Gottfried even calls him Tristan's father outright.[4] He was this legally in that Tristan was an orphan, and symbolically too once Tristan became his liegeman and heir. But above all affectively a maternal uncle was "even more than a father" in those parts and those times.[5] Add to this that a proxy father's wife is a proxy mother, and Tristan's amour with Isolde was Freudianly bound to end in grief. In a late medieval variant, jealous Mark himself kills his offending more-than-son, usually by a thrust to the groin. But the milder Mark preferred by Thomas and Gottfried is all too long either duped or compliant, with Tristan succumbing instead to one of a series of sex wounds from the fearful giants he keeps running through.

Isolde is equally a mother figure for Tristan in the other Celtic germ of his legend. In it she nurses him, a maternal function par excellence. Since the verb "to nurse" has the same two meanings in Old French as in Middle to Modern English, that equivalence of healing Tristan's wound with suckling him does not turn on the word itself. Pushing it, Thomas gave Isolde a homonymic mother to do the nursing, a queen radiant like herself to the point of sameness, celebrated in Gottfried's lovely lyrics as "Isolde wise, Isolde fair, / Who glistens like the morning air."6 Thomas even doubled the twice-motherly nursing. First, his Tristan slays an Irish giant, mother Isolde's brother, who has been holding England tribute, but thereby receives a wound that she alone can cure; he approaches her incognito and displays such refinement that she cures him "for the sake of my daughter," who would learn the courtly arts from him.7 Second, he later returns to Ireland to woo that fair princess for King Mark and kills a dread dragon on arrival; the two Isoldes find him overcome by its fumes; the mother nurses him back to health, this time while the daughter tends him; he thereupon confounds a false claimant to his doughty deed, then accepts for Mark instead of himself the posted reward of the princess's hand. True, young Isolde meanwhile discovers in Tristan her uncle's slayer and brandishes his own sword against him, which is hardly motherly of her. But he is even then being bathed like a baby in her care, and "her womanly nature" stays her brandishing hand.8

Once these two Celtic kernels of the legend fused, much local folklore was grafted onto them, first in Britain and then across Europe, as Tristan's renown spread. Brittany adopted Tristan as a native son and contributed a ravishing Isolde Whitehands for him to marry when he sails home from England to his Breton domain as a fugitive from Mark's mounting suspicions. Traditionally this second duplicate Isolde fell to his matrimonial lot when he vanquished a powerful local lord bearing his father's name who wanted her for himself. With this Freudian subplot worked into it, the Freudian plot proper thickened. It thickened further when Thomas, hard upon noting that "this tale varies a good deal,"9 gave it a whimsical twist of his own whereby the lovelorn newlywed Tristan caresses Isolde Fair in effigy in a cave while begging off from sex with her live Breton replica because of a genital wound incurred in slaying an African giant. The incest with Isolde proper being tabooed with her Breton twin: by the time Thomas wrote, this much and no more of his warped Breton triangle was stock Tristan lore, with the spurned spouse turning against Tristan in the end and this cross-Channel Isolde split thus resembling the one between Tristan's good and his evil father, alias Mark and the monsters. As if this were not Freudian enough, Thomas topped it off with that "lifelike"[10] make-believe Isolde in the cave (a third duplicate Isolde: first came mother Isolde, then wife Isolde, and now mannequin Isolde) and especially with the sex wound that his Tristan puts between himself and the flesh-and-blood surrogate Isolde in bed with him. This wound points backward and forward at once. It redoubles the low blow already dealt Tristan by his Irish giant, wherewith in his riposte the tip of his Freudian sword had snapped off for good measure. It also anticipates his fatal gash in the groin from a Breton giant whom he later slays for taking captive the "beauteous beloved"[11] of a duplicate Tristan incongruously nick-named Dwarf Tristan. Meanwhile he forgets his sex wound when he explains his wife's inviolate maidenhead to his brother-in-law exclusively by his love for Isolde Fair.[12] But he never forgets that Isolde Fair's equal love for him does not spoil her fun in bed with Mark: "From him [she] has her desire," he laments.[13] After putting Tristan through 644 verses of inhibited lust beside his frustrated Breton bride,[14] Thomas sums it up simply: "He has a wife he cannot lay."[15]

That "cannot" answers to either meaning Freud attached to impotence: mother fixation or castration fear.[16] Indeed, the Europe-wide developments of the Tristan saga depart from Freudian orthodoxy, if at all, no further than for the Breton Tristan to slay his father's slayer or for the Byelorussian Tristan to behead a castrating princess.[17] For the rest, all known versions are Freudianly at one—over and beyond the insistent parricide, incest, and castration—in representing Tristan's forbidden love as a curse gratified only at great peril and with deep guilt. The Freudian payoff is a symbolic homecoming to the womb: though Tristan meets his death without Isolde, she fast follows, enfolding his dead body from head to foot. In a tack-on by Thomas elaborated by his successors, outgrowths of their two corpses intertwine.[18]

As has been amply shown, both Thomas and Gottfried toed this traditional Freudian line all the way and even stretched it some. At the same time, though, they, and they alone, fitted Tristan's story out with a whole new motivational lining on top of the old one.[19] And not only was the received subtext for the Tristan legend what Freud thought it was for Sophocles' *Oedipus the King*; the subtext superadded by Thomas and Gottfried to the Tristan legend was like the one superadded to the Oedipus legend by Sophocles except that, where Sophocles' Oedipus contrives to relive the traumatic exposure that followed his birth, Thomas's and then Gottfried's Tristan reaches still further back into his history to relive instead a tragic love whence he had issued.

This tragic love relived by Tristan was that of his father, Rivalin.[20] A budding knight from Brittany, Rivalin does a stint abroad in Mark's famed retinue to enhance his courtly prowess. The grand and winning figure he cuts there ("never was a stranger more loved"[21]) enraptures Mark's sister, peerless Blancheflor, whose exceeding beauty inflames him in return. As her lofty rank puts her beyond his proper reach, the two flirt in secret until Rivalin is critically wounded in a tournament (Thomas) or while fighting invaders (Gottfried). Blancheflor sneaks into his sickroom with her nurse's connivance, swoons into his bed, and conceives. He recovers, only to be called back to Brittany by warfare on his domain. He cannot remain at Mark's court much longer anyhow (Thomas), nor can Blancheflor (Gottfried), without disgrace or worse, so she elopes with him to Brittany. There he weds her with great ceremony, installs her with his marshal's wife, and rides off to his death in battle. She agonizes for three days, then bears a son and expires. This birth is trauma-induced[22]: at the dire news about Rivalin, "deadly pain so gripped her heart that she bore Tristan . . . and herself died of it."[23] The marshal has his wife stage a brief confinement so they can pass the baby off as their own lest the French king (Thomas) or a hostile overlord (Gottfried) have it killed to avoid an English claim on the fief. They christen it Tristan, meaning Man of Sorrow.

That grievous conception and birth were Tristan's evil fate, sealed at his christening by a name chosen to express them[24] as well as, Gottfried adds, the sad life that was thereby "given him to live."[25] This child of a deathly love thus follows in his father's tragic train as he in his turn goes from Brittany into Mark's service, wins Mark's trust and affection while excelling in courtly skills and graces, but then enters into an unlawful, clandestine liaison with the first lady of the realm, one clouded by sorrow from the start and destined to end in the lovers' death. Like father, like son.

Actually Tristan does not so much pursue his patrimonial fate as it pursues him. Fate takes him from Brittany to Mark's court in the first place when some pirates kidnap him only to dump him ashore in Cornwall just where Mark's hunting party happens to be passing. In Thomas's account, fate later steers his bark to the double Isolde in Dublin when he sails off aimlessly to die of his wound from the Irish giant; Gottfried, though, had him do that steering himself. And that evil fate is still astir when, at the last, his wife, Isolde Whitchands, tricks him into thinking that Isolde Fair is not coming to cure him, the parental payoff being that he succumbs to his wound and Isolde Fair duly dies of grief afterwards.

Fate is restlessly astir in Gottfried's rhetoric. Does Isolde the Irish queen's daughter chance to catch sight of Tristan overcome by the stench of his slain dragon? Not all that simply, as per Gottfried: "It now came to pass, as it was meant to and as fate willed, that the young Queen Isolde was the first to espy her life and death, her joy and sorrow."[26] For Gottfried, the parental tragedy itself followed fatefully from Blancheflor's love cure of Rivalin wounded unto death: from Rivalin's sickbed Blancheflor "bore death away with her,"[27] this then being "the death she begot with the child."[28]

Above all, fate in Thomas and Gottfried alike assumed the guise of the love potion inadvertently drunk by Tristan and Isolde together. Mother Isolde, who knew her herbs, had mixed that brew for conjugal bliss. Not because it induced love, then, but because it signified Tristan's fatedness to relive his parents' tragic love in particular, did that concoction itself contain "the lasting sorrow . . . of which they both would die."[29] Isolde's maidservant Brangane, remiss custodian of the treacherous flask, is a knowing instrument of fate: "Oh woe, Tristan and Isolde," she cries when the damage is done, "this drink will be the death of you both!"[30] Tristan himself, mortally poisoned by his Breton giant's sword, yet tells his brother-in-law: "The brew was our death . . . in the hour when it was given us we drank our death."[31] Isolde accentuates love only unto, rather than into, death in assuring Tristan as he exiles himself from suspicious Mark's realm: "One body, one life, are we."[32] But then, sailing to Tristan where he lies dying, she tells him instead from afar: "You cannot die without me, nor can I perish without you."[33] Finally, in a touching last utterance beside his corpse she uses his very word, "brew," for the love philtre: "[Having] come after your death, I draw comfort from the same brew!"[34] This unwitting echo from an Isolde fulfilling Tristan's fate clinches the potion's symbolic value.

But Tristan also lends fate a strong hand in replaying his father's illicit romance. After having only chanced to join King Mark's court as a lad, he rejoins it deliberately as a young man, leaving his Breton affairs in the marshal's care as his father had done before him. He sells a reluctant Mark on Isolde as a one-and-only: Mark had wanted to stay single so as to keep Tristan as his sole heir. Only after Tristan pulls off Mark's suit against all odds, with Isolde duly betrothed, does the elixir come in. With Isolde Whitehands he likewise replays the parental misadventure on his own hook, in simple turnabout: he does companionate knightly service to a Breton ruler's son whose sister he then weds without sex.

It remains that an outer fate carries him "home without his knowing it"[35] to "his unsuspecting father"[36] in the first place. Unlike Oedipus, who has every reason to suspect his father in King Laius when he betakes himself to Thebes, Tristan has no reason to suspect a more-than-father in King Mark when he is abducted and cast ashore in Cornwall. He first learns his parents' real identity and sad fate when the marshal runs him down in Mark's court after a three-and-a-half-year man-hunt up and down western Europe. Thomas's Tristan only weeps for pity like the rest of Mark's entourage at the marshal's disclosures about that tortured parentage.[37] But Gottfried's Tristan is hard hit to learn that he has no father[38] (he ignores his having no mother). Does this blow perhaps set him reliving the rest of his father's fate after coincidence has brought him to Mark's court in his father's footsteps? That could explain why later, instead of just drifting like Thomas's Tristan, Gottfried's sails straight to the two-in-one Isolde who will heal his wound[39]—except, alas, that the marshal's disclosures skip over the parental precedent, Blancheflor's love cure: as far as either Thomas or Gottfried indicates, Tristan is never aware of this key piece of the tragedy he relives. Or perhaps Blancheflor's love cure was bruited about in Cornwall or Brittany, with those two bards merely neglecting to say so? Even then Tristan would still die before Isolde not by his own devising, but by her Breton double's treachery,[40] nor would Isolde die right after him except for having drunk of that sad cup of fate.

In sum, neither Thomas's nor Gottfried's Tristan stage-manages his whole reliving as Sophocles' Oedipus does his; rather, the necessity that Tristan acts out is internal and external combined. Thomas's and Gottfried's other, older subtext, the family romance, also works by enchantment, with kidnapped Tristan finding his way home to his royal more-than-father not just unknowingly, as Gottfried stresses, but involuntarily—unlike Oedipus rushing headlong on his own steam from Delphi home to Thebes. For all their grandeur and subtlety, Thomas and Gottfried preserved not only the chimeras of mythic thinking (sphinxes or dragons), but also, unlike Sophocles, its simplistic supernaturalism, with happenstance underpinning their hero's purposes all along his predestined way. In an equally un-Sophoclean vein, Tristan relives not an experience of his own, as does Oedipus, but his father's experience leading up to his conception and birth—an experience about which he learns only incompletely at that, from hearsay midway through his faithful reliving of it. Gottfried is explicit, moreover, about Tristan's reliving and its blindness both: he calls the paternal original of Tristan's dire fate his "hereditary pain"[41] and speaks of his "hereditary love" for Isolde.[42] For all its primitiveness by Sophoclean standards, this extension of the medieval hereditary principle to cover reliving a parental trauma strikes an arrestingly modern note.

In fond, false remembrance, Thomas's dying Tristan fits his reliving to the paternal original all too snugly in bidding his emissary to remind Isolde "of our perfect and true love when she cured me of my wound."[43] This reminder, off the mark for Tristan's double cure by duplicate Isolde in Dublin, is right on target for Blancheflor's love cure of Rivalin—which love cure Isolde then repeats in the negative when she dies coddling dead Tristan.[44] Indeed, whereas Blancheflor conceived on her first night with Rivalin, Isolde remains barren through years of sex with her two men by turns, as if saving herself maternally to enfold dead Tristan like a baby in the end.

The gorgeous refrain of Tristan's tragic reliving is the love song by which he woos and wins Isolde Whitehands even as in his heart he sings it to his own Isolde Fair:

> Îsôt ma drûe, Îsôt m'amie,
> En vûs ma mort, en vûs ma vie![45]

As Gottfried twice gives this exquisite lyric in French, it would seem to be of Thomas's making. Thomas approximates it twice in the extant fragments, each time using a singular verb for the two maternal legacies in one: "The fair queen, his love, in whom is his life and his death,"[46] and elsewhere "in whom his life and his death rests."[47] Gottfried himself reechoes it continually on the order of "Tristan's life and his death, his living death, Isolde Fair."[48] Only because of his fated reliving were Tristan's life and death thus personified by Isolde fronting for his mother. For all her seeming self-will, Isolde is a mere instrument of Tristan's reliving, condemned to die of grief once he succumbs to a battle wound: that, and no lovers' parity, is why "one death and one life . . . was given to them both,"[49] or again why "the death of both, the life of both, they were as woven into one."[50] "Woven into one": only in a later century that eroticized death could a Richard Wagner make over that curse whereby Isolde died "of grief for her lover . . . because she did not come in time"[51] into an ecstatic *Liebestod*.

Thomas's and then Gottfried's two subtexts were as one in requiring a tragic outcome. In their two texts, as in the whole Tristan corpus, that fatality was ascribed to the unlawfulness of Tristan's and Isolde's love. Not to its wrongness before God: God's one big showing in Thomas or Gottfried is to support Isolde's "trickery"[52] in an ordeal testing her fidelity to Mark. But despite this divine boost, the lovers' transgression against the earthly social and moral order cannot go unpunished indefinitely: their wiles and dodges only delay the final reckoning. The more they elude discovery, the more they suffer inwardly from their offense against Mark and, still worse, against a code of rectitude that they themselves accept. Their tragedy was always and everywhere sung with sympathy for them trapped inside their wicked passion, and increasingly with a wistful indulgence for that passion itself as opposed to drab duty denying it free rein. This unresolved conflict between the claims of duty and those of love heightened the melancholy suffusing the legend from first to last.

In presenting that conflict, while Thomas psychologized more and Gottfried philosophized more, they both put a distinctive edge on the received moral of the tale. In Béroul and Eilhart, as in their sources, Tristan's and Isolde's guilty passion was like a poison inflaming the senses beyond all normal human measure. But for Thomas and Gottfried, that guilty passion was simply unbridled love. For them, not just evil love presses against the social and moral order; love itself does at its gut level. Society must work by rules; emotion, though, is inherently rash and unruly, especially so imperious an emotion as love. Society in Thomas and Gottfried is an intricate complex of prescriptive usages and reciprocal obligations, with only a tenuous hold on raw human impulses. Conversely, pure love as brewed by mother Isolde is inimical to any and all control or constraint. Let out of its flask, it bursts all courtly and humane bonds to press for consummation as a matter of life and death. "We are dying of love," Tristan tells Isolde's maid in Gottfried when the potion is drunk[53]—and, urging her to let them love in secret, "Our death and our life are now in your hands."[54] This echoes Blancheflor's drastic appeal to her nurse, prompted by no magic potion, to sneak her into Rivalin's sickbed: "Help me or I'm dead!"[55]

Imperative, love is also selfish, antisocial, in Thomas and Gottfried alike. The more lovers love each other, the more heedless they are of others. But they cannot live by love alone. Rivalin and Blancheflor, off all by themselves in their stolen "true love,"[56] know a "worldly joy entire"[57] only until its time runs out. In every extant version Tristan and Isolde flee the world once for a forest idyll that proves unviable: they either cannot survive without society or else society drags them back.

Society apart, love as seen by Thomas and Gottfried destroys itself anyhow in due course. The wages of its thrills is its torments. It makes those smitten with it possessive and suspicious, deceptive and self-deceptive. Thomas, an expert on love's inner destructiveness, rhymes *amur* with *dolur* incessantly right down to his closing couplet. Gottfried set his lovers' forest idyll, or "dream life,"[58] in a pagan love cave, love's harmony there being the very measure of its disharmony elsewhere. His tolerance of suffering for passion's sake was higher than that of Thomas, amounting to outright advocacy at times. But his characters knew better. His Blancheflor rebuked love for luring us "with passing joy to lasting sorrow."[59] As for his Tristan, "Loyalty and honor both tried him hard, but love tried him harder. It gave him more pain than pain itself and brought him more sorrow than loyalty and honor combined."[60] Gottfried's sagest advice was worldly-wise, with a touch of levity: to spite love by at least enjoying its snares. But this is just what Thomas's and Gottfried's Tristan, doubly driven, can least of all Tristans do.

NOTES

1. Béroul, *Tristran*, 1789–90: "as the story says where Béroul saw it written" ("conme l'estoire dit, / La ou Berox le vit escrit").

2. For these, see Gertrude Schoepperle, *Tristan and Isolt: A Study of the Sources of the Romance* (1912; 2nd ed., New York: Burt Franklin, 1960).

3. The legendary names vary from one version to the next. I am using those most current in English.

4. Gottfried von Strassburg, *Tristan*, 3382: "der . . . vater sîn."

5. Letter from Georges Duby, 10 January 1995. On this age-old special bond, cf. Tacitus, *Germania*, 20: "A sister's sons are as much honored by their uncle as by their father; some even hold this blood tie to be closer and holier" ("Sororum filiis idem apud avunculum qui ad patrem honor; quidam sanctiorem artioremque hunc nexum sanguinis arbitrantur").

6. Gottfried, 7291–92 (literally, like the flush of dawn: "diu wîse Îsôt, diu schoene Îsôt / diu liuhtet alse der morgenrôt").

7. Friar Róbert, *Tristrams saga ok Ísöndar*, chap. 30; cf. chap. 32. This is an authoritative if somewhat condensed Old Norse prose translation of Thomas dated 1226. About one-fifth of Thomas's original survives in five discontinuous, corrupt fragments that dovetail with Gottfried's unfinished work to end the poem.

8. Friar Róbert, *Tristrams saga*, chap. 43. (She then stays the queen's hand—and the queen next stays hers in turn.)

9. Thomas de Bretagne, *Tristran*, 2104 ("cest cunte est mult divers"); further, ibid., 2110–12; Gottfried, 131–54. For convenience I am citing Thomas's lines as numbered in Stewart Gregory's Thomas of Britain, *Tristran* (New York: Garland, 1991); cf. Thomas, *Le roman de Tristan*, ed. Félix Lecoy (Paris: Honoré Champion, 1991).

10. Friar Róbert, *Tristrams saga*, chap. 80.

11. Thomas, 2208 ("bele amie").

12. Ibid., 2522–23 ("Itant aim Ysolt la reïne / Que vostre suer remaint mechine").

13. Ibid., 154 ("de lui ad sun desir"). Further, ibid., 225–35: he wants to marry not to get even, but to find out what it's like for her.

14. Ibid., 54–697.

15. Ibid., 1114 ("Feme a a qu'il ne puet gesir").

16. Sigmund Freud, *Gesammelte Werke*, vol. 8 (London: Imago, 1943), 79, 82, or vol. 14 (1948), 170.

17. *The Byelorussian Tristan*, trans. Zora Kipel (New York: Garland, 1988), 118–20. (Probably the phallic lady derived from Tristan's African giant, who cuts off his victims' beards.)

18. Friar Róbert, *Tristrams saga*, chap. 101 (not in Thomas's fragments); Schoepperle, 65. A later Spanish ballad substituted a single plant such that "any woman who eats of it promptly feels pregnant" ("cualquier mujer que la come / luego se siente preñada"): *Spanish Ballads*, ed. C. Colin Smith (Oxford: Pergamon, 1964), 187.

19. By all indications Thomas devised this second subtext, which only Gottfried then took up. Béroul's *Tristran* and Eilhart's *Tristrant*, which both postdate Thomas, evidently ignored it (the relevant opening section of Béroul is missing, and Eilhart survives only in tiny fragments, bad rewrites, and a dubious Czech translation).

Subsequent medieval and Renaissance Tristan literature followed Eilhart and Béroul rather than Thomas and Gottfried.

20. In Eilhart's *Tristrant* with its strictly Freudian subtext, Tristan's father shares this name with the rival whom Tristan vanquishes to win Isolde Whitehands.

21. Gottfried, 513 ("enwart nie gast geminnet baz").

22. Ibid., 1741–54, 4205–12; cf. Friar Róbert, *Tristrams saga*, chap. 15.

23. Gottfried, 4208–12 ("diu tôtlîche swaere / sô sêre ir in ir herze sluoc, / . . . / daz sî den [Tristan] von der nôt gewan / und lac sî selbe tôt dervan").

24. Friar Róbert, *Tristrams saga*, ch. 16; Gottfried, 1983–2022.

25. Gottfried, 1991–2012 (2011–12: "sehen wie trûreclîch ein leben / ime ze lebene wart gegeben"). In this prophetic verse the marshal is reminiscent of the oracle at Oedipus's birth.

26. Ibid., 9369–74 ("nu ergieng ez, alse ez solte / und alse der billîch wolte, / diu junge künigîn Îsôt / daz sî ir leben unde ir tôt, / ir wunne unde ir ungemach / ze allerêrste gesach"): note the conflation of mother and daughter in the designation "the young Queen Isolde."

27. Ibid., 1338 ("truoc mit ir von dan den tôt"); 1317–40: for Rivalin too the lovemaking is as deathly as it is restorative.

28. Ibid., 1340 ("den tôt sî mit dem kinde enpfie").

29. Ibid., 11674–76 ("ez was diu wernde swaere, / . . . / von der si beide lâgen tôt").

30. Ibid., 11706 (11705–6: "ouwê Tristan und Îsôt, / diz tranc ist iuwer beider tôt!").

31. Thomas, 2492, 2494–95 ("El beivre fud la nostre mort / . . . / A tel ure duné nus fu / A nostre mort l'avum beü").

32. Gottfried, 18344 ("ein lîp, ein leben daz sîn wir").

33. Thomas, 2910–11 ("Vus ne poez senz moi murrir, / Ne jo senz vus ne puis perir").

34. Ibid., 3108–9 ("venue sui a la mort, / De meïsme beivre ai confort!"); cf. Thomas, *Le roman*, 3110 ("de meisme le bevre avrai confort"). "Brew" is admittedly odd, but it is distinctive like "beivre."

35. Gottfried, 3379–80 ("Nu Tristan der ist ze hûse komen / unwizzende").

36. Ibid., 3382 (Mark = "der unverwânde vater sîn").

37. Friar Róbert, *Tristrams saga*, ch. 24: Tristan's only special reaction is to "wish . . . to avenge the death of my father."

38. Gottfried, 4227–32, 4367–77.

39. Ibid., 7400–7402.

40. This treachery is due to jealousy of Isolde and hence indirectly to the love potion, yet in no wise is it Tristan's doing.

41. Gottfried, 19127 ("erbesmerzen").

42. Ibid., 19179 ("erbeminne").

43. Thomas, 2488–89 ("De nostre amur fine e veraie / Quant el jadis guari ma plaie"). Oddly, though in Thomas "he had no physician but the queen" (Friar

Róbert, *Tristrams saga*, chap. 38), when the princess threatens him with his sword he already reminds her wrongly that *she* has twice saved him from death (chap. 43)—a confusion doubtless due to the textual doubling of the single subtextual Isolde. But there is no trace whatever in Thomas of any "perfect and true love" between them then.

44. Gottfried jocularly brought Isolde's tragic end closer to Blancheflor's strenuous love cure by saying that Rivalin, already a "dead man" before ("mich toetet dirre tôte man," says Blancheflor: 1230), would then have succumbed except for God's help (1328–29).

45. Ibid., 19213–14, 19409–10. Stretching "m'amie," one might venture: "Isold' my love, Isold' my wife, / In you my death, in you my life."

46. Thomas, 1062–63 ("La bele raïne, s'amie, / en cui est sa mort e sa vie").

47. Ibid., 2709 ("En qui maint sa mort e sa vie").

48. Gottfried, 18467–68 ("Tristandes leben und sîn tôt, / sîn lebender tôt, diu blunde Îsôt").

49. Ibid., 11443–44 ("in was ein tôt unde ein leben / . . . samet gegeben").

50. Ibid., 14331–32 ("ir beider tôt, ir beider leben / diu wâren alse in ein geweben").

51. Thomas, 3119–21 ("Pur la dolur de sun ami / . . . / qu'a tens n'i pout venir").

52. Gottfried, 15742 ("trügeheit").

53. Ibid., 12111 ("wir sterben von minnen").

54. Ibid., 12117–18 ("unser tôt und unser leben / diu sint in iuwer hant gegeben").

55. Ibid., 1225 ("dune helfes mir, sô bin ich tôt").

56. Ibid., 1362 ("lêal amûr").

57. Ibid., 1369 ("werltwunne vol").

58. Ibid., 16846, 16872 ("wunschleben").

59. Ibid., 1409 ("mit kurzem liebe ûf langez leit").

60. Ibid., 11767–72 ("in muoten harte sêre / sîn triuwe und sîn êre. / sô muote in aber diu Minne mê, / diu tete im wirs danne wê. / sie tete im mê ze leide / dan Triuwe und Êre beide").

5

Lust Forever
Dante's *Inferno*—The Francesca Episode

Comedy was Dante Alighieri's title for his poetic masterpiece that Boccaccio called divine and that a reverent posterity, outdoing Boccaccio, later retitled *The Divine Comedy. Inferno*, the first third of Dante's *Comedy*, was circulating by 1314. In it Dante recounts his imaginary midlife tour of hell guided by dead Virgil, who was afterwards to conduct him through purgatory and then to turn him over to blessed Beatrice, flame of his youth, for a climactic ascent through paradise. *Inferno* has at all times been cited and discussed more than its two sequels, *Purgatory* and *Paradise*, put together. And the seventy-odd lines of it dominated by the person and story of Francesca da Rimini have proved incomparably the most memorable passage of the whole sublime poem, inspiring derivative works of literature, music, and art galore alongside of commentary unending.

This Francesca sequence of *Inferno* tops off Dante's fictive visit to the second circle of the underworld as he envisioned it in a rich personal construction on the orthodox view of his day. The first and outermost circle, called "limbo," is a mere benign border region—a belt of verdant meadowland peopled by unbaptized infants and virtuous pagans in painless gloom. Dante's hell proper begins only where Francesca is confined: in the second of the nine concentric subterranean circles that converge on Lucifer at their dead center. In this hell proper, according to Dante's very Christian conception, unrepented sinners relive forever the mortal sins that define them; indeed, those defining sins are revisited upon them with a punitive twist. The mildest of the four sins of incontinence is the one being relived in Francesca's circle: lust. On penetrating this circle Dante learns from his pagan cicerone, Virgil, that it holds "carnal sinners, who subject reason to desire,"[1] and Virgil points out among them "over a thousand" historic or legendary slaves of passion.[2] These swarms of damned sinners are literally reaping the whirlwind, for their earthly lust torments them incessantly in the form of fierce winds that keep blowing them round about with no hope of respite. Stunned and distressed at this spectacle with its attendant chorus of groans, Dante fixes on one male and one female shade who, tempest-tossed together, yet seem to be flying "light upon the wind."[3] He bids them come and speak to him and Virgil. Here is what then follows, with Dante's verse form sacrificed for accuracy in translation: "As doves beckoned by desire, with wings raised and firm, come to the sweet nest, borne through the air by their will, so these [two] left the swarm where Dido[4] is, coming to us through the baleful air, so forceful was my fond cry. 'Oh live one gentle and kindly, who goest through the dark air visiting us who stained the world with blood, were the king of the universe our friend we would pray to him for thy peace since thou pitiest our woeful fate. Of that which thou art pleased to hear and speak we shall hear and speak with you [both] while the wind is quiet here. On the shore where the Po descends to rest with its tributaries lies the town where I was born. Love, which spreads quickly to the noble heart, smote him there with the fair form that was taken from me; and the manner still afflicts me. Love, which absolves no one loved from loving back, smote me so strongly with pleasure in him there that, as you see, it still does not leave me. Love led us to one death: Caina[5] awaits him who quenched our lives.' These words were borne from them to us. When I heard those injured souls, I bowed my head and held it down until at length the poet said to me: 'What art thou thinking?' When I replied, I began: 'Ah me, how many sweet thoughts, how much longing, brought them to this sorry pass!' Then I turned to them and spoke, and began: 'Francesca, thy torments make me weep for sorrow and pity. But tell me: in thy time of sweet sighs, by what and how did love grant you [both] to know your latent desires?'[6] And she to me: 'No pain is greater than to recall in misery a happy time; and this thy teacher knows. But if thou art so eager to know our love's first root, I shall tell like one who weeps in telling. One day we were reading for pastime how love constrained Lancelot. We were alone and wholly unsuspecting. Several times our reading drew our eyes together and took the color from our faces, but at one point alone did it defeat us. When we read of a coveted smile being kissed by such a lover, he here, who is never to be parted from me, kissed my mouth, all trembling. A Galeotto was the book and he that wrote it[7]: that day we read no farther in it.' While the one spirit said this, the other so wept that I fainted for pity as if I were dying and fell as a dead body falls."[8] Dante's swoon in the windy second circle of his hell terminates his interview with Francesca and simultaneously the fifth of the hundred cantos of his *Comedy.*

Stripped of its poetry, this brief Francesca episode is puzzling in lots of ways and not a little silly. A first problem with it on a naïve reading is that it does not divulge how the narrator knows his interlocutress's name. Before he calls her Francesca, all that she tells him specifically through her fancy periphrases is that she was born in Ravenna and was murdered together with her lover. Even Rimini, at once her married name and her place of death, goes unmentioned. Nor does she identify herself any more closely when, speaking a second time, she relates the circumstances of her precipitous slip into sin. Yet at the start of the next canto the Tuscan tourist in hell calls the two inseparable souls he has just left behind brother-in-law and sister-in-law.[9] Did he recognize Francesca physically from real life even without her recognizing him in return, and even with her "fair form" taken from her? Then the one-way acquaintance was a strangely close one, and he ought not to have been so exercised by a personal history that can have been no news to him. In point of fact, real-life Dante never set eyes on real-life Francesca, whose husband, lord of Rimini, caught his married younger brother, Paolo, in bed with her and cut them both up some thirty years before that passage of *Inferno* was penned. Dante's Francesca alludes to this fratricide in the manner of an insiders' guessing game through the words "Caina awaits him who quenched our lives."[10] Conversely, she omits from her high-blown self-presentation any and all hint that her deadly liaison was adulterous. Perhaps Dante as author wished to avoid the appearance of confusing the second circle's sin of sex for its own sake, namely lust, with its sister sin of illicit sex. But adding adultery to her vita would not have helped much to distinguish Francesca anyway.

Problematical too are the terms of Dante's exchange with Francesca if they are taken at face value. His single question to the pair of airborne lovers is a loaded one: by what and how they became aware of their latent desires. The question presupposes that they had harbored amorous designs on each other without knowing it until some shared self-disclosure. This gratuitous assumption passes unnoticed because Francesca does promptly relate just such a shared self-disclosure. Only she introduces her account of it with the remark "But if thou art so eager to know our love's first root," whereas neither their love as such nor still less its first root is what her questioner has asked about, nor indeed is either what she then tells him about. Rather he has asked, mincing his words, how love gave way to lust, and she replies by blaming Lancelot so touchingly that the whole lusty sequel is conclusively forgotten, its duration unknown.

Anomalous above all in this interchange is the figure of ladylike Francesca with her unladylike boldness. Dante bids the two "wearied souls" come and speak to him and Virgil. At this bidding, Francesca puts herself forward as if by rights to answer alone for her partner as well as herself. Filling the scene with her person and recollections, she addresses Dante exclusively, ignoring Virgil except for a token plural "you" at the outset, while her pale wimp of a supposed seducer so weeps beside her that Dante passes out from pity. To compound the anomaly, with this strong showing from Francesca comes a plea of fatal weakness as she claims that love undid Paolo and her in quick succession, then blames gallant Lancelot in a French romance of the day for having pointed them on their wanton way. She sounds her plea through a magniloquent recitation that contrasts pointedly in style with the simple, straightforward narrative mode of the poem, suggesting a studied, self-serving monologue. However artfully devised and delivered, her claim against love in that pit of lust should fool no one, though it clearly takes her impressionable questioner in. The blame she levels against "such a lover" as Lancelot for his wicked example is the flimsier since it was actually coquettish Guinevere who, in the incriminated French romance, had coaxed a first kiss out of that Arthurian warrior. Francesca switches the amorous initiative to Lancelot in citing this analogue to her own case. Was Dante, who knew his French romances, here tacitly impugning Francesca's good faith? Hardly, or her pathos would not have confounded him with such grief as he afterwards remembers that it did.[11]

Francesca's plea of weakness, spelled out in full, is that her mortal traffic with Paolo was a misadventure from first to last—that she was more sinned against than sinning or, worse, was acted upon while herself only helplessly reacting. But her professed victimization by life flies in the face of the very facts she imparts in professing it. In the first of her two pat speeches she welcomes Dante's pity for the "woeful fate" that befell her lover and herself, expatiates on her birth for no discernible reason except that it was preeminently none of her own doing, and then charges love in three successive stanzas (the word itself opens each of the three) with smiting Paolo's gentle heart, and through his gentle heart her own, only to prove the death of them both in the end. In her second, closing speech she charges that French tale about how love constrained Lancelot with having prompted faint Paolo, all atremble, to kiss her mouth, thereby setting the rest of her resonating. But if, as she asserts, uninvited passion did sweep the unsuspecting pair away in an unguarded moment, then they do not belong among the "carnal sinners, who," in Virgil's foregoing, authoritative formulation, "subject reason to desire," for such subjecting must needs be consenting. In churchly talk befitting Dante's day and age, an urge is not imputable if it is not controllable. Was Dante as author imagining a miscarriage of the divine justice he was at such pains to vindicate in his whole *Comedy*? Or is his Francesca striking a false moral pose that Dante as the compassionate pilgrim of the *Comedy* fails to see through?

No matter: by Francesca's own say-so, passion carried the lapsing latent lovers away only as far as a kiss. From that kiss to her bedroom, and thence down to the bloody end of their intrigue unnumbered days and kisses later, "reason" had time enough to intercede. "That day we read no farther," says Francesca, as if the all-out adultery followed automatically and for the indefinite future once Lancelot had broken the gentility barrier and their lips had met by enchantment. True, Dante sets Francesca up to focus her exposé of her sin on its beginnings with the built-in implication that, once under way, it was all of a sequential piece. Francesca then in her turn more than obligingly puts the sinner's familiar spin on sin as developing out of its origins by an inner fatality like a sickness rather than being a series of discrete free acts. But besides the logic of her story, the force of her assertive personality rules out her having lost her power of choice once and for all in helpless compliance with her reading partner's timid love. If anything, pathetic Paolo could pass for her victim more easily than she can for his.

Over and beyond Francesca's own special pleading, the poet props up her pose of passivity by lending her entire episode a passive cast. The two lovers glide over to the inquiring visitor in the first place not of their own volition, but on the wings of his desire to hear them—and yet, in a bafflingly contradictory simile, like doves borne by their own desire. Straightaway the stranger to hell falls under Francesca's spell: that sympathetic defenselessness befalls him which she claims befell her following Paolo's kiss. After her first speech he wonders with tender solicitude what sweet thoughts and longings first led the damned couple into mortal sin. His phrasing here accords with hers in that he puts the two lovers in the tow of their sweet thoughts and longings, quite as if those sweet thoughts and longings were having them instead of the other way round. Nor does he ask Francesca all that directly "by what and how" she and Paolo came to know their latent desires; his question is rather "by what and how" *love granted them* to know their latent desires. By this point Francesca has already convicted love in the abstract of ensnaring Paolo and, through him, herself. When she now denounces the French romance for having drawn their latent desires out of them, Paolo sobs—whether from pity for her, himself, or both, at all odds with their live visitor now in that passive posture toward her that she claims had been hers toward Paolo. That visitor thereupon closes the reactive circle around her by fainting for pity at Paolo's sobbing.

But the forced reactivity contextualizing Francesca's two set pieces also surrounds her with a vengeance in that spooky second circle swarming with lusty souls hurled about by tempestuous winds. This penalty for lust is a drastic metaphor of its practitioners' having abandoned themselves to carnal passion during their mortal incarnations—or, in this infernally timeless takeoff on earthly life, for their abandoning themselves to carnal passion now and forever at a single crucial moment, like swimmers yielding to a deadly undertow. In Francesca's and Paolo's shared case, this literalized metaphor looks at first blush more like a privilege than a punishment. If lust is indeed their vice, should not the two lovers clasped forever in each other's fleshless arms prefer even this counterfeit of passion to lonely salvation? Why then do "thy torments," as the impressionable outsider puts it to Francesca, make him weep? Not even Tristan, whom Virgil points out in the second circle before Francesca appears, is favored there with the proximity of his life's and death's mate.[12] Francesca's indifference to her silent partner weeping beside her—in her speeches she expends all her commiseration on herself and denotes Paolo only by trivializing, even slighting, demonstratives[13]—might suggest that she has tired of him over their fifteen-odd stormy years together down under[14] except that Dante's hell is of all places the one where nobody ever changes.

Just about any one of these problems of consistency and meaning in that fifth canto could undo a lesser passage of a lesser work. But such a rundown of textual troubles with this grand Francesca scene rings false. Francesca's story as told by Dante, its infernal sequel inclusive, has resounded down the ages even outside of Italy, with its poetry largely lost in translation. There must, then, be more to it than meets the eye if what does meet the eye is flawed and its meaning confused. What is that more?

To find out, let us hark back to Francesca's account of how her intimacy with Paolo started. For memory, Dante asks "by what and how" their love ever became conscious. Francesca says that it did so by the force of Paolo's feeble kiss, which she calls their love's "first root," and she adds with a suggestiveness just a trifle infernal: "That day we read no farther." The implication is that the adultery promptly sprouted from its first, wild root as a natural, organic outgrowth requiring no consent from her in the process. This implication falls in with her earlier talk of love coercing her. It falls in too with the tempest of the second circle forever tossing the lovers about, this being figurative, I repeat, of their surrender to their carnal impulse that fateful day and ever after. Yet Francesca does not come across as one to react mechanically. Lust would not have subdued that proud soul definitively at a jittery kiss from Paolo whether she only returned it or instead, like Lancelot's Guinevere, even elicited it. Her twofold feeble excuse for her sin—that love spreads quickly to the noble heart and that it absolves no loved one from loving back—overstates her sentimental vulnerability without, however, drawing any sensual, let alone any venereal, consequences from it. Not even by her own testimony, then, was she lost to lust once Paolo fretfully kissed her mouth.

But if she did not yet lust at that kiss, when did she? The answer glares forth from between Dante's lines. Later, as Paolo's eager mistress, Francesca necessarily knew at the very least one recurrent moment of self-surrender to lust: that moment when the sex act, pressing to a climax, takes on a momentum of its own—when lovers go from persons interacting to flesh of each other's flesh, from having sex to its having them. This is the existential point at which, subtextually, Dante's damned souls in his second circle are all suspended. Those winds wildly blowing them "back and forth, up and down,"[15] eternalize just that sexual crescendo hellishly intensified, yet bereft of carnality and hence forever incapable of completion. Francesca, slain in Paolo's arms, personifies that eternalized moment of climactic unfulfillment. For just that reason—her death in the act, at the telltale psychological moment—is she in particular spotlighted in that pit of lust.

That psychological moment in turn is why the way in which Francesca's body was taken from her in Paolo's embrace "still afflicts" her. Whatever this cryptic utterance of hers means textually—the usual reading is that, caught in the act, she was slain too fast to repent, although conversely she is still impenitent fifteen-odd years of eternity later—as subtext it is graphic. That psychological moment of devouring self-absorption through the medium of a lover also explains why Paolo, nominally a full partner in love, is such a shadowy shade in this scene stolen by Francesca—why she upstages and depersonalizes him both at once. Heedless of that unnamed and unheard accessory in lust even while protesting that she loves him still, Francesca exemplifies a love that has spent itself, if indeed it was ever love at all. Loveless sex, not unrepented adultery, is her ticket to that billowy and blustery second circle; the concomitant adultery is a technicality that her lust, like Dante's narrative, can do without. Because passion rules the souls stuck in that lusty circle, all action there is the reaction that it was in life: this, then, is why Francesca talks only in terms of being acted upon, including her projective construction on Lancelot's kiss.

Back to that kiss that Guinevere actually wrests out of Lancelot in their romance. It is Francesca's excuse for Paolo's kiss, itself in turn her excuse for kissing Paolo back: to this apologetic effect she misconstrues Lancelot as a bold, forward lover with Guinevere. In her tearful, tricky version of her mortal lapse she displaces it upwards from the epicenter of her lust to her mouth kissed by Paolo and thence to Guinevere's smile kissed by Lancelot. Her stilted, periphrastic diction is the language of concealment that reveals. Love mastering her through Paolo's kiss, as she depicts her fall, fronts for her willing subjection of spirit to flesh afterwards at the orgasmic moment, or in fact for her willing that moment itself repeatedly on its own account. To lust is to crave extinction of the mind and the will, of the partner and the self, in sheer fleshly animality—a Christian synonym for spiritual death.[16] It belongs to Dante's subtext that love pushes for sex, which then threatens love. And it belongs to his text that "love" is Francesca's cover word for lust, just as in Francesca's second speech the lovers' losing control after their eyes meet over Lancelot's kiss is a screen for their losing control at closer quarters later along. To take this cover word of Francesca's, echoed by her live visitor, *alla lettera* is to forget where in hell she is, let alone that her author has singled her out to quintessentialize her circle's sin. For the author of *Inferno* saw straight and deep, whereas its main actor of the same name begins his tour of the underworld impressionable to a fault, and nowhere more so than in this early Francesca episode.

The force of Dante's poetic art comes of his integration of text and subtext such that neither works without the other, whereas both work wonders together. The anomalies that abound in his text emerge when, and only when, it is lifted out of its poetic frame. Within that frame they convey a subtext that blends into the text to intensify its overall effect. In the text Francesca is in hell for lust as if by mistake and is seemingly favored with her beloved's perpetual company. In the subtext Francesca has lusted rather than loved, whence she is being punished by her ill-loved partner's perpetual company in permanent excitation without respite or release. How this subtext blends into this text has been shown only disjointedly, so it bears reviewing summarily point by point. That Francesca, while wholly feminine, yet visibly holds her lover in thrall speaks to the intimate place where medieval women, exalted in courtly love only at their men's discretion, did exert momentary control—"where their husbands are most subservient," to quote a medieval farce.[17] Francesca's claim that erotic compulsion set in with Paolo's trembly kiss evokes, with a deft touch, the fleshly juncture at which sexual compulsion did later set in. Francesca relates that her reading together with Paolo brought out their love; the prose to this poetry is that their love brought out their lust. The subtextual moment of lust shapes Francesca's rhetoric of reactivity and Dante's concordant setting for her two speeches. Her lust shows most starkly through her genteel talk of her "pleasure in him," with that "him" denoting the pathetic nobody at her side. Finally, Dante's assumption that the twosome's desires were latent before some occasion brought them out unresisted falls into place as the Christian doctrine of potential sin. For defilement comes of no French romance, but— and this is gospel—"from within, out of the heart."[18]

One textual problem remains: that of Dante the character all too readily recognizing Francesca in the second circle. Did the author Dante foresee that, thanks to the huge popularity of his Francesca scene, his posterity too would recognize her as soon as she appears?

Of all the abundant art, music, and literature drawn from this arresting Francesca episode, Ingres's 1819 painting of the seduction scene between the lovers is the most celebrated single item. Ingres did violence to Francesca's story as told in the *Comedy*, yet he made the same implicit point as Dante by means of a single, simplistic, melodramatic image. Dante's evasive Francesca, in telling her tale, avoids suggesting how long her affair with Paolo had lasted before her body was taken from her. But when, in explicating her amorous beginnings at Dante's request, she says that she and Paolo read no farther after Paolo's Lancelot-like kiss, she indicates none too subtly that their intimacy began only after that reading. In reality they were stabbed to death in her bed, hence indeed crucially later than their first kiss. Ingres, however, so construed Francesca's euphemism in the *Comedy* about their having read no farther that day that on his canvas Francesca's warped and wicked husband advances from behind a curtain, rapier in hand, just as Paolo bends timorously forward to kiss not even her mouth, but her cheek, while she sits with the chivalric French romance dropping from her hand. The lovers are decorously clad; Paolo is rapturously transfixed; Francesca is not even reactive, let alone coactive, but just languorously unresisting. Ingres's Francesca and Paolo were, then, to be left high and dry by their impending murder, their love forever unconsummated. This composition, on the surface a near travesty of Dante's poem, nonetheless converged with it on the subsurface level of the lovers' eternalized suspense on the verge. The painting combines into a single, refined image the lovers' self-surrender to carnal desire and their eternal, infernal arrest at that point of surrender. One deft detail: whereas in Dante's poem their reading of the French romance repeatedly draws the lovers' eyes together, in Ingres's painting Francesca's gaze, dreamily averted from Paolo, falls instead where her limp arm and index finger point: toward the French romance that has turned them on. However shy or sentimental, love divorced from its object, as in that gaze of Francesca's, tends to lust. And that is where, at Dante's infernal level, all love tends. In Ingres, at least Dante's Christian moralism, if not his visionary genius, survived.

NOTES

1. Dante Alighieri, *La divina commedia*, V:38–39.
2. Ibid., V:67–68.
3. Ibid., V:75.

4. Virgil's Dido broke faith with her dead husband for love of Aeneas, then killed herself when Aeneas deserted her.

5. The ring of central hell for traitors to kin.

6. "Latent desires" sounds wrongly protopsychoanalytical, but it exactly renders Dante's "i dubbiosi disiri," desires dubious or questionable because still unexpressed.

7. Gallehault was Guinevere's go-between with Lancelot in the French romance. His name in Italian came to mean "pander" (which comparably anglicizes Pandarus, legendary go-between for Troilus and Cressida).

8. Dante, V:82–142.

9. Ibid., VI:2.

10. See n. 5. Caina is evidently named for Cain, who slew his younger brother.

11. Dante, VI:2–3.

12. After Francesca's and Paolo's murder the rumor arose that their love had begun when Paolo went to Ravenna to negotiate Francesca's marriage on his kinsman's behalf. Was this rumor inspired by the Tristan legend?

13. "Costui" ("him there") twice, "questi" ("he here") once.

14. The *Comedy* is set in the year 1300.

15. Dante, V:43.

16. Romans 8:6: "To set the mind on the flesh is death."

17. *Quinze joyes de mariage*, quoted by Erich Auerbach, *Mimesis* (1946; Princeton, NJ: Princeton University Press, 1968), 251 ("là où leurs mariz sont plus subjets").

18. Mark 7:21 (7:15–23).

6

Strange Mutations
Shakespeare's *King Lear*

World, world, O world!
But that thy strange mutations make us hate thee
Life would not yield to age.[1]

Edgar, hero of the subplot of Shakespeare's *King Lear*, speaks these lovely lines about strange mutations upon catching sight of his father just blinded and being led away from the family castle. It strains credulity for Edgar to be philosophizing at this juncture about the normal process of growing old. But his words are no easier to penetrate if they are seen or heard out of context. "Life would not yield to age" is generally taken to mean that one would not resign oneself to growing old. I read Edgar as saying, more ambitiously, that one would not grow old at all—that senescence is not built into life but comes of the continual shakeups to which life is subject. Either way, there is a problem of internal consistency in what Edgar says. For life does yield to age in the end, as Edgar indeed allows in that very statement. Those strange mutations must therefore be in steady supply. But by the very force of the term "strange mutations" they violate the normal course of things. How, then, can they be in steady supply? Elsewhere Edgar is high on natural process. For its sake he tricks his father out of committing suicide, then puts it that he "saved him from despair."[2] Next, when his father feels too weary of life to flee before a hostile army, Edgar gorgeously insists that one must die only as one is born, in the natural course, despite any suffering involved: "Men must endure / Their going hence even as their coming hither: / Ripeness is all."[3] Some lines later,[4] even as he warms up to recount his father's "miseries," he forgets these so far as to claim that we do naturally cling to life despite all the agony it may involve: "O! our life's sweetness, / That we the pain of death would hourly die / Rather than die at once!"[5] Were this sweetness so, the world's strange mutations could not resign us to aging and dying, although alternatively they might wear us out. Given these crossed indications, to fuss over how these strange mutations relate to the natural course of life in Edgar's and, once removed, Shakespeare's view of it may seem idle. My excuse is that the normalcy of strange mutations, that conundrum in Edgar's utterance quoted in epigraph, is at the textual level the thematic crux of *King Lear* as a whole.

In *King Lear* a run of strange mutations convulses a kingdom initially at peace with itself, leaving a mere couple of survivors fit to restore order afterwards. In plot and subplot alike the trouble starts with a father rashly turning against a cherished child as a result of a false appearance. In the plot old King Lear proposes to parcel out his realm into dowries for his three daughters if they will say ceremonially "Which of you . . . doth love us most."[6] The two eldest, Goneril and Regan, both already married, duly fawn on Lear in state. But then "our joy" Cordelia, as Lear calls her,[7] will not play along. Stung by this seeming disaffection, Lear switches Cordelia's portion to her sisters and banishes a loyal courtier, the Earl of Kent, for protesting. The French king gallantly takes Cordelia to wife dowered only with Lear's curse,[8] and she departs for France commending her father to her sisters' "professed bosoms."[9] Promptly Lear's counterpart in the subplot, the gullible Earl of Gloucester, is tricked by his bastard, Edmund, into having his loving legitimate son and heir, Lear's godson Edgar, pursued for an alleged parricidal intent that is at bottom wicked Edmund's own. As Edmund boasts, his "practices ride easy"[10] on his half brother as well, who falls right in with the flimsy frameup of him contrived by Edmund.

Mighty convulsions ensue. Cordelia's sisters on their side, and Edmund on his, soon swing around from declared filial love to deadly hate—unlike Cordelia and Edgar, who manage to love only the more for being wronged. Legitimate turns illegitimate as Lear and Gloucester are themselves outlawed after they outlaw Kent and Edgar—as the proscribers are proscribed. Power turns to impotence by the same token. Kent, disguised as a rustic servingman, spends a night in the stocks, while Edgar is driven to impersonate a Bedlam beggar for dear life; Gloucester is blinded and "thrust . . . out at gates,"[11] while Lear roves a storm-swept moor homeless, his bearings lost. More dizzying still are the concomitant ups and downs of status. Edmund usurps his father's estate on his way to supplanting both Goneril's and Regan's husbands before—in his own imagery—the wheel comes full circle.[12] Conversely, Kent plunges from comfortable courtier to fake menial before rebounding. Edgar is obliged "To take the basest and most poorest shape / That ever penury, in contempt of man, / Brought near to beast,"[13] only to wind up ruling the realm. The biggest comedown grandly reversed (with a couple of flips at the last) is Lear's from commanding majesty to a fugitive madman who tears his clothes away as he cries: "Off, off, you lendings!"[14] pending his restoration to "absolute power"[15] even in defeat and captivity just before his heart breaks. More in Lear's wider province of "the mystery of things,"[16] sane and insane change off. Philosophical Edgar enacts mad Tom with panache. Lear acquires wisdom in losing his wits. The Fool regularly speaks sense through nonsense. Blasting age-old standards of seriousness in drama, the action scales its highest heights of significance with a royal lunatic, a professional half-wit, a bogus hireling, a make-believe madman, and a blinded outcast "blown unto the worst"[17] on a tempestuous heath.

Not just on that tempestuous heath is nature a party to the human convulsions in *King Lear*. Early along, Gloucester foresees "all ruinous disorders"[18] following from the stars: "Love cools . . . there's son against father . . . there's father against children."[19] Kent agrees in retrospect: "The stars above us govern our conditions."[20] Lear is less merely reactive to nature, more interactive with it, than these two dukes. Crossed by his elder daughters, he sumptuously announces deeds of revenge that "shall be / The terrors of the earth."[21] "Contending with the fretful elements"[22] out on the moor, he "Bids the wind blow the earth into the sea . . . / That things might change or cease"[23] and "Strives in his little world of man to out-storm / The to-and-fro conflicting wind and rain."[24] Upon taking shelter, he rages on about "this tempest in my mind."[25] But not only do specific characters in *King Lear* make sky-high and worldwide issues of their personal affairs. Shakespeare himself typically cast such dire fates as Lear's in terms encompassing an unexampled wealth and variety of phenomena natural and unnatural, of sentiments human and inhuman, of modes from the lyrical and sublime to the prosaic and rough-hewn, of genres from pure tragedy through morality play to melodrama and farce. The effect in *King Lear* was to open out its existential upheavals in all directions even while its main action seesaws between sheltered castles and "the tyranny of the open night."[26]

The theme of turnabouts, a blatant lesser sort of strange mutations, is explicit, even insistent, throughout *King Lear*, resonating like a leitmotif from phrase to phrase: "thou madst thy daughters thy mothers"[27]; "the cart draws the horse"[28]; "a man's brains were in's heels"[29]; "look with thine ears"[30]; "we'll

go to supper i'th'morning"[31]; and "I'll go to bed at noon."[32] Less playfully, when
Goneril's husband says that her steward "turned the wrong side out" in lauding
Edmund's usurpation,[33] Goneril resolves like a carnival queen, or a feminist
before the fact: "I must change arms at home and give the distaff / Into my
husband's hands."[34] Akin to such turnabouts are interchanges of high and low
symbols (crown and coxcomb[35]) and alternances of high and low diction. Amid
this ever-broadening, ever-quickening whirl of shakeups and switchoffs, Lear
stages a mock trial of his daughters as if to create order out of chaos, while
Edgar on the contrary twists the laws of nature "above all strangeness"[36] to have
Gloucester fall on level ground as if from a sky-high cliff in Dover. At length
the mad king sees "how this world goes"[37] as that it goes topsy-turvy. A man
flees a barking watchdog? "Behold / The great image of authority: / A dog's
obeyed in office."[38] As to the moral order, wrong infests the great image of
right, the law courts: "Robes and furred gowns hide all."[39] "See how yon justice
rails upon yon simple thief . . . change places and, handy-dandy, which is the
justice, which is the thief?"[40] Images apart, wrong is right turned inside out.
"Thou rascal beadle, hold thy bloody hand! / Why dost thou lash that whore?
Strip thine own back. / Thou hotly lusts to use her in that kind / For which
thou whipst her."[41] That this world goes topsy-turvy means above all that
appearances conceal and hence mislead. They expressly do so in mad Tom's
handy-dandy diabolism with its bottom line: "The Prince of Darkness is a
gentleman."[42] But before that they have already done so to touch off the whole
run of strange mutations in *King Lear*: when Cordelia and Edgar are victimized
by false appearances to which the audience is cued in.

    Strange mutations and, to keep them coming, false appearances: these were
not Shakespeare's concern alone in his time. The world destabilized by strange
mutations in *King Lear* imaged the world destabilized in men's thoughts by a
convulsive crisis of doubt then raging across Europe. This crisis, the birth pains
of modernity, arose over the knowability of anything. The new science taught
that all appearances were false in that the sensory qualities of things are supplied
by the perceiver. But the new science did not yet teach the means of circum-
venting perception. Hence reality was regarded as elusive, perhaps illusory. The
great, and beguiling, exponent of such radical uncertainty in literate England
at the time of *King Lear* was an outsider: Michel de Montaigne, translated into
English by Shakespeare's friend John Florio in 1603. For *King Lear*, which
followed within two years or so, Shakespeare took numerous grand passages
fairly straight from Florio's Montaigne, including Gloucester's and Kent's
words on the stars, Edgar's on reason in folly, and Lear's on garments as
lendings, on sham justice, and on handy-dandy.[43] But Shakespeare outdoubted
Montaigne himself. Where Montaigne found a refuge from skepticism in

exploring the one thing he felt that he could know directly and indeed inside out, his own self, Shakespeare in *King Lear* focused most sharply of all on personal identity as subject to strange mutations that called its very existence into question.

Lear harps on the theme of personal identity as if to make sure it duly registers. When on Goneril's orders her steward comes "slack of former services" to him,[44] Lear asks: "Who am I, Sir?"[45] and explodes at the answer: "My lady's father."[46] He taunts Goneril by demanding: "Are you our daughter?"[47] and "Your name, fair gentlewoman?"[48] Of his party he inquires: "Does any here know me?"[49] and "Who is it that can tell me who I am?"[50] (The Fool quips in reply: "Lear's shadow."[51]) On first seeing disguised Kent, Lear exclaims: "How now! what art thou?"[52] and Kent answers: "A man, sir."[53] Remotely echoing Kent (as well as Montaigne), Lear cries in tearing off his clothes on the moor: "Thou art the thing itself; unaccommodated man is no more but such a poor, bare, forked animal as thou art."[54] In this creatural perspective to which Lear without his crown attains, individual identities are themselves like disguises— like counterfeits. That is why mad Lear, fantastically bedecked with wild flowers, declares: "No, they cannot touch me for coining. I am the king himself."[55] His mock trial of his daughters parodies the concept of identities outright. Calling poor Tom "most learned justicer"[56] and the Fool "sapient sir,"[57] then the two respectively "robed man of justice"[58] and "his yoke-fellow of equity,"[59] and enjoining disguised Kent in turn: "You are o'th' commission. Sit you too," he orders: "Arraign her first: 'tis Goneril."[60] The Fool complies, addressing a joint-stool: "Come hither, mistress. Is your name Goneril?"[61] Lear interjects all too accurately: "She cannot deny it."[62] With that, the Fool exclaims to the joint-stool: "Cry you mercy, I took you for a joint-stool."[63]

Personal identity mutates in *King Lear* most obviously through classic disguises. The play features two major classic disguises, which would be two too many for a tragedy without that main theme of strange mutations. "Enter Kent, disguised"[64] heralds a turnabout full spiral downward as the king's noble servant, "banished Kent,"[65] reappears, his "likeness" "razed,"[66] to do the king "service / Improper for a slave."[67] And Edgar in turn, on hearing himself "proclaimed"[68] (outlawed), assumes "a semblance / That very dogs disdained,"[69] enabling him to bear up his blinded father and, retailored, cut down his upstart half brother. Against all odds, both masqueraders go unrecognized on a theatrical license.[70] Both also tarry overlong in impostures that transform them inwardly, each in his own way. Kent's false face and accent metamorphose him from an urbane, upright liegeman to Lear into a boisterous, pugnacious, rambunctious troubleshooter. Undisguised again, he falls, "tranced,"[71] into a deathly sorrow from recounting the king's trials even before the fatal finale. At the last, declining to rule with Edgar, he goes off wistfully to die instead, aged only forty-eight.[72] Edgar for his part is clearly more in his element in the person of poor Tom philosophizing darkly than earlier in his own "foolish honesty."[73] His Bedlam act brings out his affinity for masks, all his denials to himself notwithstanding. Chameleonlike, he assumes three supplementary disguises in a row before he is done, impersonating by turns a fisherman who gathers up Gloucester after Gloucester's false leap from Dover cliff, a peasant who protects Gloucester from Goneril's steward out to slay him,[74] and a mysterious avenger who exposes first Goneril's plot against her husband's life and then Edmund's villainy. Unlike Kent, he leaves off playacting matured rather than aged, and incomparably strengthened: he shapes up masterful and decisive after having started out as his half brother's facile prey.

Edmund's mutations are all in the moral figure he cuts. They are strange to his kinsmen. They are not strange, though, to the reader or spectator alerted by his soliloquies—not, at any rate, until near the last. The play opens with his father, Gloucester, bantering in his presence while waiting for Lear to hold court: "This knave came something saucily to the world before he was sent for, yet was his mother fair; there was good sport at his making, and the whoreson must be acknowledged."[75] After presenting that whoreson to Kent, Gloucester concludes: "He hath been out nine years, and away he shall again."[76] Here, then, from the word go, is motivation aplenty for Edmund's seeking to "top th'legitimate" Edgar,[77] for his pursuing his father with a vengeance, and for his using adultery to advance his cause. His repentance as he dies by Edgar's hand is a complete, albeit a conventional, turnabout. But he also mutates strangely in the process as he exults at the sight of Goneril's and Regan's corpses: "Yet Edmund was beloved."[78] The rejected child had craved love before revenge, and now, repentance be damned, he savors it briefly in extremis before he remembers, too late, Cordelia in the wings being hanged on his orders.

Stranger by far to their entourages and their audience both are Lear's daughters' moral mutations. His two elder daughters, Goneril and Regan, are not simply wicked from all time, fairy-tale-like, as is commonly held. Rather, their wickedness toward him, toward their sister, and toward each other emerges progressively in that order, with their personalities changing apace. Nor is their wickedness arbitrary; on the contrary, Shakespeare motivates it as fully as he does Edmund's in the parallel subplot, only he does so more by implication, through evidence of its origins that is visible as soon as the scene is set. Actually the specificity about Edmund's motivation is limited to the stigma of bastardy rankling him, whereas his soliloquies leave what drives him hardest unexpressed: his mortal enmity toward a father able to chuckle cavalierly within earshot of him about, in his half brother's words, "The dark and vicious place where thee he got."[79] Here too, plot and subplot run parallel. Just as Edmund's reckless "making" was the point of departure for his fierce hostility toward his father, so does Lear's daughters' deep and deadly filial spite go back to the circumstances of their own begetting.

Consider, as if on opening night, that fateful scene introducing the royal family. The king is pronouncedly aged; later he will say that he is "fourscore and upward," adding whimsically: "not an hour more or less."[80] By contrast, his daughters are strikingly youthful—hardly over twenty, and all three close in years. For traditionally a make-believe princess's bridal age was roughly twenty, and Goneril and Regan, while no newlyweds, have not been married long enough for their childlessness to be an issue. Thus the picture emerges at a glance of a king who was pushing sixty when he married—and who was sexless otherwise, for no bastard of Lear's steps forth as does Gloucester's whoreson a moment earlier in the parallel subplot. The simple indications are that the king took a young wife late in life just to get a male heir, and that he lost her trying or else a fourth child would have followed. She must have been beautiful to attract him, as are all her daughters. She would have been less than royal, however, for the kingdom he parcels out is legendary Albion complete from way back, with no addition from her dowry. That he considers Cordelia unmarriageable once he rescinds her portion of the realm—one of her two suitors, Burgundy, does promptly beg off—points back to a presumable low regard for his own landless wife. His bribing his daughters to show him affection is suggestive of how he dealt with their mother. In the entire play he mentions his lost queen only once, to say that her tomb would be "sepulchring an adult'ress"[81] should Regan not be glad to see him; no heartfelt remembrance by him, this is rather a mere theatrical ploy to signify that she was dead and buried. He adverts to her indirectly when he raves against her sex: "Down from the waist they are centaurs / Though women all above."[82] Her failure to produce a male heir can only have lowered his esteem for that childbearing vessel still further. He would make up for this disappointment by demonstrative doting on his daughters topped off by his incautious resolve to award them his kingdom in his own lifetime. Such compensatory affection went above all to Cordelia as his last-born, who may have cost her mother's life. Because it is compensatory, that perfervid fatherly love is fragile, as shows in his hasty, nasty rejection of Cordelia in the busy opening scene. This background all looms behind that one scene, however hazily, with no need to search it out.

The dead queen lives on through her elder daughters' avenging her against Lear. It is no mere accident of medical vocabulary that Lear calls the choking rage these daughters arouse in him "mother"[83] and admonishes it: "Thy element's below."[84] He defeats his own purpose when he throws his parenthood at them time and again ("my flesh, my blood, my daughter"[85]) while leaving their mother's parenthood out of account. They have each evidently played for his favor from the first ("They flattered me like a dog," he recalls in madness[86]) with retribution obscurely in mind, yet also with enough hankering after his scant affection mixed in for their rivalry to prove deadly when it refocuses on Edmund. They turn the parental tables on him vicariously in that they boss their husbands[87] with a vengeance that also proves murderous. They meanwhile replay their mother's debased conjugal role in the negative by failing to conceive.[88]

Outwardly, however, Goneril and Regan have, like Cordelia, been their father's rather than their mother's children until the division of the kingdom. Lear fully expects and trusts their declarations of daughterly love at the opening ceremony, for he has mapped out their "ample"[89] portions in advance and even throws in Cordelia's in a huff. So they have played up to him convincingly all their lives. Behind his back they do not fool each other about only playing up to him; as Goneril tells Regan, Lear's poor judgment in having cast off Cordelia in their favor "appears too grossly."[90] Nor do they fool Cordelia, who remarks in a parting shot at them: "I know you what you are."[91] But Cordelia cannot yet know the whole deep, dark, deadly truth about them any more than they themselves know it; her prophecy to them that "Time shall unfold what plighted cunning hides"[92] says as much, for all its ominous irony. Their tête-à-tête after she goes, with Goneril urging Regan: "Pray you, let us hit together,"[93] shows no frankly evil sisters scheming to undo Lear, but just wary, selfish, unloving daughters fretting over what is now in store for them from the trying monarch. Not without cause: after two weeks of hosting Lear and his "insolent retinue,"[94] Goneril complains, with the ring of truth from her vantage point, that "His knights grow riotous, and himself upbraids us / On every trifle."[95] When at her bidding "a little to disquantify your train"[96] Lear curses her with grim ferocity and storms off to Regan's, Goneril sends ahead so alarmingly about his "riotous knights"[97] that Regan flees her castle at his approach. The strange mutation that both elder sisters undergo together thereafter can be measured in Goneril's case by the distance that her husband, Albany, traverses between remarking to her at this juncture on "the great love I bear you"[98] and later calling her "devil,"[99] "gilded serpent,"[100] and "worse than any name."[101] Albany is even explicit about her metamorphosing in that he later also styles her a "changed and self-covered thing."[102] Whatever he means by "self-covered," it neatly suggests layers of externality. The changed sisters stop shedding these layers only when the one finally poisons the other and stabs herself.

Somewhat unlike her elder sisters, baby Cordelia would have had little or no chance to identify with her mother directly. Yet in her defiant refusal to fawn on Lear ceremonially for her dowry, she shows a provocative harshness that does not jibe with her earlier loving asides, let alone with her later risking and losing her life for him only a fortnight after he has cut her off with a "curse" and an "oath."[103] Her statement, purportedly from the heart,[104] for the regal occasion of the division of the realm amounts to a decorous slap in the face: "I love your Majesty / According to my bond; no more nor less."[105] It does serve one positive purpose for her as she faces betrothal: it severs for the foreseeable future her all-too-close tie with her father even in mislabeling that gut bond as duty only. But above all, it conveys some of the same deep-rooted animus against Lear that forms the core of her sisters' personalities while not being integrated into hers.

That Shakespeare meant ambivalent Cordelia's pretended candor as sauciness—as a strange mutation of her accustomed sweetness—is clear from his later parody of the episode of the award of the dowries. In the event Kent reacts against Lear's "hideous rashness" toward Cordelia,[106] and later toward him as well, by telling her in open court that she has "most rightly said"[107] where an apology for her petulance would have been more to the point. But then that same Kent, while disguised in Lear's service, stages in Gloucester's castle a clownish pastiche of the falling out between Cordelia and Lear. Echoing at once both Cordelia's claim to have been simply honest, or "true," rather than "untender" with Lear[108] and Lear's stricture on Cordelia's "pride, which she calls plainness,"[109] Kent tells Regan's husband in coarse accents: "Sir, 'tis my occupation to be plain," and proceeds to give gratuitous offense: "I have seen better faces in my time / Than stand on any shoulders that I see / Before me at this instant."[110] Regan's husband thereupon mocks Kent in terms appropriate to Cordelia's boast about herself: "he cannot flatter, he, / An honest mind and plain, he must speak truth: / And they will take it, so; if not, he's plain."[111] Kent in reply mimics Goneril and Regan next, affecting high-blown flattery in courtly diction beginning: "Sir, in good faith, in sincere verity."[112] Challenged on this performance in turn, Kent protests yet again: "I know, sir, I am no flatterer," adding that he would not be one "though I should win your displeasure to entreat me to't"[113]—which throws back to Cordelia's priggish plea to Lear to tell France that she has fallen into disgrace and disfavor for want of "such a tongue / That I am glad I have not, though not to have it / Hath lost me in your liking."[114] Rounding out the replay, Gloucester intercedes for Kent in vain just as Kent himself had interceded for Cordelia in vain.

Kent's burlesque gives the measure of Cordelia's offense that unhinges Lear and that she afterwards passes off to France as a mere want of her sisters' "glib and oily art / To speak and purpose not."[115] Unhinged, Lear declares: "I loved her most, and thought to set my rest / On her kind nursery,"[116] and later: "we / Have no such daughter, nor shall ever see / That face of hers again."[117] That he does see that face of hers again and does set his rest on her kind nursery for a brief moment before the tragic finale is the central turnabout of the play. It is in no small measure Cordelia's own turnabout—away from pride and back to tenderness.

For all that, Cordelia changes least; Lear himself it is who changes most. Indeed, Lear changes drastically from scene to scene, and sometimes even within scenes. Lear at the last would be unrecognizable from Lear at the first except that we see him pass, often abruptly, from one cast of soul to another as he reaps the wild wind he has sown. Within one rough night all his feelings toward the world at large converge into a monomaniacal rage against Goneril and Regan; both demonic daughters promptly cease to exist for him, however, when Cordelia reappears the next morning and he falls into a childlike love of her excluding every other emotion, his sudden childish "hate" for her[118] having been lost in the shuffle. During his rage he inches into madness, thundering gigantically all the way, only to reemerge "a very foolish fond old man,"[119] submissive and subdued, until at Cordelia's death his fury flares up anew, this time beyond his sapped strength. In going mad he typically goes into reverse. Sexless when sane, he is sex crazed when mad, then again pure of mind and heart as if purged. Shortsighted when sane, he turns sharp-eyed in madness, whereafter his vision literally fades. In the thick of his madness he suddenly slips out of self-pity into compassion for "Poor naked wretches, whoso'er you are,"[120] and then right back again. His imperious self-will yields by fits and starts to a final humility that yet harbors grandiosity at the heart of it. Likewise, his egocentric fury against the refractory world passes over into a gentle endurance with room in it still for his indiscriminate outcry when Cordelia dies: "A plague upon you, murderers, traitors all!"[121] In view of these number-less inner shakeups, it is not enough to say that Lear changes beyond recognition. The point is rather that, except in bodily externals, there is no single, hard-and-fast, self-identical Lear who wrestles with his self-inflicted fate. Even at age eighty and upward, the personal entity Lear is volatile, discontinuous, radically mutant. After the tempest that he unleashes and weathers in his mind, he cannot recognize or remember much from before. Subjectively he retains only fragments of the disintegrated former Lear, which then reassemble in a new configuration under the same name.

Paradoxically, the single most constant fragment of the lot is also the least personal: his kingship. Chiding him over his abdication, the Fool tells him: "I am better than thou art now; I am a Fool, thou art nothing."[122] Yet even divested of office, Lear retains what disguised Kent calls "authority"[123] and again "royalty."[124] Deep in the pits, having shed his wardrobe and his wits alike, he no less remains, in his own words, "every inch a king."[125] This inveterate royal air that ever envelops his shambles of a self is what made *King Lear* rather than just *Lear* the unmistakably right title for the play.

Just as his huge inner convulsion leaves Lear humbled when its tremors die down, so does his kingdom lose his autocratic impress as it passes into disarray and at length rearray. With the initial political and moral order in Albion falling into chaos, the fabric of life as a whole unravels in five agitated acts; then, as the boards are cleared of corpses, it promptly reweaves itself under Lear's shaken successors Edgar and Albany. Edgar remarks in closing that "the oldest hath borne most."[126] Indeed, in Lear and Gloucester, both of them irrepressibly lively greybeards just days before, life has yielded to age in full, while Kent too, lately stalwart and prankish in his prime, is fast succumbing. But the recent epidemic of strange mutations has scarred the next generation as well. For Edgar adds: "We that are young / Shall never see so much, nor live so long."[127] Never see so much: has Edgar outspoken himself? Upsets such as only just shattered the realm are unforeseeable; otherwise they would be less traumatic, less tragic. Mutations natural to the world are strange to us: such is the resolution of the conundrum in Edgar's utterance quoted in epigraph. The last word on such unsettlings, however resettled, was already spoken by Gloucester before Edgar's peroration: "This great world / Shall so wear out to naught."[128] The way from Edgar on mutations to his father on entropy, from the world aging us to the world wearing out, from my epigraph to this epitaph, is a short and straight dead end.

That this great world is unfit for human habitation is the shrill subtext of *King Lear*. The tragedy is not specific to its victims, as was an Oedipus's or a Tristan's fate,[129] or just to one realm, as when a Troy is sacked or a Thebes maddened; it inheres in the whole of creation. Nor is the trouble moral. Old Gloucester does pay too cruelly for his putdown of Edmund, Lear for his tyrannical doting, Cordelia for invading her homeland, but all that is only incidental. In *Othello*, written just before *King Lear*, the trouble was moral: that mean Iago could trick grand Othello into strangling chaste Desdemona puts life itself to shame. The overtheme of *Othello* comes into *King Lear*: that nothing is what it seems. The Moor himself is at once noble and ignoble, wise and foolish, savage and tender. Lear is likewise ambiguous, or at all odds a changeling. But the tragic undertheme of Lear's story is metaphysical, not moral: that the laws of being are, like the storm on the heath, unlivable—that "man's nature cannot carry / Th'affliction nor the fear."[130] And that, on Edgar's say-so as I read it, is why we grow old and die.

This undertheme of the play accords with its overtheme of strange mutations. It accords as well with the plethora of loose ends in the plot[131] and the frenetic tempo between the serene opening of the action and the final calm of exhaustion. Above all, it speaks to our universal buried fear that the world might run down or run amuck. That fear makes tragic sense.

NOTES

1. William Shakespeare, *King Lear*, IV.i.10–12. Editions of *King Lear* vary in minute particulars of styling. In my citations I have tried to observe the most usual spelling, punctuation, and line numbering.

2. Ibid., V.iii.189.
3. Ibid., V.ii.9–11.
4. Ibid., V.iii.179.
5. Ibid., V.iii.183–85.
6. Ibid., I.i.51.
7. Ibid., I.i.82.
8. Ibid., I.i.203.
9. Ibid., I.i.272.
10. Ibid., I.ii.178.
11. Ibid., III.vii.92.
12. Ibid., V.iii.173.
13. Ibid., II.iii.7–9.
14. Ibid., III.iv.107.
15. Ibid., V.iii.298.
16. Ibid., V.iii.16.
17. Ibid., IV.i.8.
18. Ibid., I.ii.113.
19. Ibid., I.ii.106, 109, 110.
20. Ibid., IV.iii.33.
21. Ibid., II.iv.277–78.
22. Ibid., III.i.4.
23. Ibid., III.i.5–7.
24. Ibid., III.i.10–11.
25. Ibid., III.iv.12.
26. Ibid., III.iv.2.
27. Ibid., I.iv.168–69.
28. Ibid., I.iv.221.
29. Ibid., I.v.8.
30. Ibid., IV.vi.151.
31. Ibid., III.vi.82.
32. Ibid., III.vi.83.
33. Ibid., IV.ii.9.

34. Ibid., IV.ii.17–18.

35. Ibid., I.iv.95–107.

36. Ibid., IV.vi.66.

37. Ibid., IV.vi.147, 150.

38. Ibid., IV.vi.159–60.

39. Ibid., IV.vi.166.

40. Ibid., IV.vi.152–55.

41. Ibid., IV.vi.161–64.

42. Ibid., III.iv.136.

43. George Coffin Taylor, *Shakspere's Debt to Montaigne* (Cambridge, MA: Harvard University Press, 1925), 9–13. Checking Shakespeare textually against Florio's Montaigne, Taylor writes: "The parallels in *Lear* . . . are, on the whole, the most striking" (9 n.4); cf. Shakespeare, *Lear*, 235–39 and passim. But only superficially do Edgar's "strange mutations" half match Florio's "ordinary mutations": ibid., 138n. Besides drawing on single passages from Montaigne, *King Lear* conveys the "full measure" of Montaigne's philosophical influence on Shakespeare: thus John M. Robertson, *Montaigne and Shakspere* (London: University Press, 1897), 135, who, however, offers no specifics. W. B. Dreyton Henderson, "Montaigne's *Apologie of Raymond Sebond*, and *King Lear*," *Shakespeare Association Bulletin* 14 no. 4 (October 1939): 209–25, and 15, no. 1 (January 1940): 40–54, bypasses the skepticism in Montaigne's most skeptical essay.

44. Shakespeare, *King Lear*, I.iii.10.

45. Ibid., I.iv.77.

46. Ibid., I.iv.78.

47. Ibid., I.iv.214.

48. Ibid., I.iv.232.

49. Ibid., I.iv.222.

50. Ibid., I.iv.226.

51. Ibid., I.iv.227.

52. Ibid., I.iv.9.

53. Ibid., I.iv.10.

54. Ibid., III.iv.104–6.

55. Ibid., IV.vi.83–84.

56. Ibid., III.vi.21.

57. Ibid., III vi.22.

58. Ibid., III.vi.36.

59. Ibid., III.vi.37.

60. Ibid., III.vi.38–39, 46.

61. Ibid., III.vi.49.

62. Ibid., III.vi.50.

63. Ibid., III.vi.51.

64. Ibid., I.iv.top.

65. Ibid., I.iv.4.

66. Ibid.

67. Ibid., V.iii.218–19.

68. Ibid., II.iii.1.

69. Ibid., V.iii.185–86.

70. Gloucester at least thinks fleetingly of his son once on seeing poor Tom (ibid., IV.i.32–34). Yet he instantly recognizes the mad king's voice as against his own son's (ibid., IV.vi.106).

71. Ibid., V.iii.216.

72. Ibid., I.iv.39; V.iii.214–17, 233–34, 319–20.

73. Ibid., I.ii.177.

74. Oddly, Gloucester does not notice the pretended fisherman's switching to peasant dialect with Goneril's steward (ibid., IV.vi.235, 237–42, 244–45) and then back.

75. Ibid., I.i.20–23.

76. Ibid., I.i.31–32.

77. Ibid., I.ii.21.

78. Ibid., V.iii.237.

79. Ibid., V.iii.170.

80. Ibid., IV.vii.61.

81. Ibid., II.iv.127.

82. Ibid., IV.vi.124–25; further, 126–27: "But to the girdle do the gods inherit, / Beneath is all the fiends'."

83. Ibid., II.iv.54. "Mother," being thought to arise from the womb, was also termed "*hysterica passio*": ibid., II.iv.55.

84. Ibid., II.iv.56.

85. Ibid., II.iv.216.

86. Ibid., IV.vi.96.

87. Ibid., I.iv.310; II.ii.132–33; cf. II,ii,150–52, 156.

88. Lear curses Goneril: "Strike her young bones, / You taking airs, with lameness" (ibid., II.iv.158–59). Her "young bones" has been construed to denote an embryo: see William Shakespeare, *King Lear*, ed. Kenneth Muir (London: Routledge, 1991), 87n. But this reading contradicts Lear's earlier invocation to nature to prevent Goneril from conceiving (Shakespeare, *King Lear*, I.iv.272–78).

89. Shakespeare, *King Lear*, I.i.80.

90. Ibid., I.i.291.

91. Ibid., I.i.269.

92. Ibid., I.i.280.

93. Ibid., I.i.302.

94. Ibid., I.iv.197.

95. Ibid., I.iii.7–8; further I.iv.196ff., 238ff., 252f., 319ff.

96. Ibid., I.iv.245.

97. Ibid., II.i.93.

98. Ibid., I.iv.309.

99. Ibid., IV.ii.59.

100. Ibid., V.iii.85.

101. Ibid., V.iii.154.

102. Ibid., IV.ii.62.

103. Ibid., I.i.204.

104. Ibid., I.i.104.

105. Ibid., I.i.92–93.

106. Ibid., I.i.151.

107. Ibid., I.i.183.

108. Ibid., I.i.106.

109. Ibid., I.i.129.

110. Ibid., II.ii.91–93.

111. Ibid., II.ii.96–98.

112. Ibid., II.ii.103.

113. Ibid., II.ii.108, 110–11.

114. Ibid., I.i.231–33.

115. Ibid., I.i.224–25.

116. Ibid., I.i.123–24.

117. Ibid., I.i.262–64.

118. Ibid., I.i.203, 210.

119. Ibid., IV.vii.60; further, IV.vii.84, V.iii.275.

120. Ibid., III.iv.28.

121. Ibid., V.iii.267.

122. Ibid., I.iv.189–90.

123. Ibid., I.iv.30.

124. Ibid., II.ii.34.

125. Ibid., IV.vi.107.

126. Ibid., V.iii.323.

127. Ibid., V.iii.323–24.

128. Ibid., IV.vi.135–36; cf. Prospero in *The Tempest*, IV.i.153–56 ("the great globe itself, / Yea, all which it inherit, shall dissolve / And . . . / Leave not a rack behind").

129. "It's mine alone, my destiny—I am Oedipus!": Sophocles, *Oedipus the King*, 1496; "sehen wie trûreclîch ein leben / ime ze lebene wart gegehen"· Gottfried, 2011–12.

130. Shakespeare, *King Lear*, III.ii.48–49.

131. Most notably, the Fool is forgotten midway, and trouble between Kent and Albany is gratuitously forecast again and again.

7

In Flames and in Tears
Racine's *Phaedra*

Racine saw the title character of his *Phaedra*, premiered in 1677, as a consummate tragic heroine in that she is "caught up . . . in an illicit passion" that horrifies her at least as much as anyone else while totally escaping her control.[1] That passion is directed to her stepson, Hippolytus, so that it is not just adulterous but also, as seen by all concerned, incestuous; hence it is unworthy twice over. Racine's drama stresses the fatality of Phaedra's passion on a near par with its culpability. It is, in a word, a curse, the preferred stuff of high tragedy in the ancient mold.

Racine took most of the plot and characters for his *Phaedra* from Euripides, who had fashioned them from familiar Greek myth. In Euripides' *Hippolytus* Phaedra's misogynous stepson, Hippolytus, shudders on learning of her love for him; in her shame and humiliation she hangs herself, leaving a retaliatory suicide note that accuses him of attempting to rape her; his father, Theseus, thereupon banishes him in such a fury that, along his way, a bull magically emerges from the sea at Theseus's bidding to chase him to his death.[2] Racine in his preface to *Phaedra* singled out three material particulars in which his rewrite of Euripides differed from the original: it decorously scaled down Phaedra's false charge against Hippolytus from attempted to intended rape; it had Phaedra's lowly nurse instead of lofty Phaedra herself level that false charge; and for Hippolytus's misogyny it substituted a "frailty" in the form of a "passion he feels, against his will, for Aricia, the daughter and sister of his father's mortal enemies."[3] This last alteration of Euripides' script reflects, at two millenniums' remove, Aristotle's felt need for some fault in a tragic hero that will prove his undoing[4]—a prescription more honored in Racine's Paris, be it noted, than in Sophocles' Athens with its tragic view that human faultlessness is more liable to offend the gods than human failing. On the other hand, Racine incongruously gave Hippolytus, and him alone, that Aristotelian-style "frailty" only to demote him from first to second fiddle. For over and beyond Racine's reworkings and refinements of Euripides' plot—there were others besides those three that he enumerated—he departed from it to focus his adaptation on Phaedra rather than Hippolytus as protagonist and victim in one. More, he imbued his Phaedra with a deadly sense of guilt over her forbidden passion instead of proud dishonor 'from Hippolytus's spurn as in Euripides. As to the playwright's and poet's craft, he dropped the goddesses and antique choruses and recast Euripides' earthy, rugged, unruly lyricism into the measured, rarefied couplets at which the French classical poets, and especially Racine himself, excelled.

Like Racine's own mastery, French classicism as a whole was then at its height, with the theater as perhaps its proudest showpiece. Its hallmarks in fiction were formal rules, purity of language, basic human significance, stylized characters, and a dearth of physical particulars, to which tragedy specifically added precise unity of time, place, and action—all in sharpest contrast to the unmistakably individual characters, abundant natural detail, and rough-hewn, sprawling, elemental matter and manner of a *King Lear*. Then likewise at its resplendent height was the Grand Monarchy of Louis XIV with its crisscross of social hierarchy and administrative leveling. Racine's typically grandiose heroes and typically universal pitch at once reflected and underwrote that absolutist intermix of vertical and horizontal.

Back to Racine's high-flung, high-strung heroine. Unlike consenting Francesca, clear-headed, high-minded Phaedra is helpless against her wicked lust. That lust, which brings on the tragedy, glows with a lurid hue right through Racine's severe propriety. The implication of its fatal hold on Phaedra is that no one, however lucid or righteous, can prevail against the enticing evil to which the flesh is heir. The author in his preface insisted that his play comes down hard on iniquity: "The passions are displayed only to show the disorder that they cause," he declared, "and vice is everywhere painted in colors that make its deformity known and hated."[5] In so saying, Racine was selling short the demonic appeal of his Phaedra's folly. At the same time, as if to redress the balance, he was understating how hard his tragedy comes down on vice and the passions: "disorder" and "deformity" sound like mere aesthetic fussing. But in any case, protest though his tragedy might against vice and the passions, its clear message was that even a Phaedra's uncommon spiritual resources are no match for them.

Never and nowhere outside of what the French call their *grand siècle*, which straddled Racine's heyday, have the passions had such a bad press. If Racine lumped them together with vice, one cause was Descartes, who convinced the French that the passions interfere with straight thinking, which of itself can never lead us into temptation. For Descartes, straight thinking even sufficed to secure virtue,[6] so that Racine departed Cartesianism to the extent that his Phaedra thinks perfectly straight but still cannot defend against her wicked will. For this departure, the decisive influence on Racine was Jansenism, which propagated among the French a direct putdown of the passions. With Pascal as its ablest exponent, this anti-Jesuitical movement within French Catholicism revivified the early Christian doctrine of a corruption inherent in the human breed that we cannot begin to surmount by our own devices, without the saving grace of God. The Jansenists did not so much scale down those devices as scale that corruption up. And so, in Phaedra's case, did Racine.

Racine's Phaedra acknowledges her corruption with mournful Cartesian-Jansenist insistence from first to last. "The gods have robbed me of my wits," she declares,[7] and again: "Reason rules no longer in my soul."[8] She terms her love for Hippolytus "my deranged craving,"[9] "my mad ardor,"[10] "[my] fury,"[11] "my crazed desire,"[12] "my wild frenzy,"[13] "my vile passion,"[14] and much more to the same tortured effect. She sees herself under the "shameful yoke"[15] of "Venus with her clutches in her prey."[16] Gorgeously she laments: "I've languished and withered in flames and in tears."[17] Ever and again she calls her pining for Hippolytus a "crime"[18] and herself "guilty."[19] She feels that guilt as a poison in her blood. Not just for baroque ornamentation is she introduced into the play as "the child of Minos and of Pasiphaë."[20] Minos was sired by Zeus disguised as a bull; Pasiphaë, grandchild of the scorching sun, lusted for another bull after bearing Phaedra, and the monstrous Minotaur was the outcome. Given her "most curst of families"[21] and her "blood . . . filled with all these horrors,"[22] smitten Phaedra longs to die before the evil coursing in her "burning veins"[23] can do its dirty work. When her nurse and confidante, Oenone, tempts her into declaring herself to Hippolytus instead of merely languishing away for decency's sake, she exclaims with voluptuous abandon: "Oenone, serve my madness, not my reason."[24] This is the point of no return in the tragic rush of events onstage, their pace forced by a classicistic unity of time and action as relentless as Racine's deadly sex goddess herself.

Racine contrived a counterpart to Phaedra's guilty love for Hippolytus in Hippolytus's guilty love for an Aricia proscribed by Theseus as the "last of a line which sought to overthrow / Our house."[25] Hippolytus writhes in self-contempt at this amorous offense against his father's will, against their common blood, and against his own cult of chastity. To his tutor, who notes his "wasting passion" all too clearly,[26] he pronounces himself defeated, degraded, humiliated by his "crazy love."[27] Avowing that crazy love to its object herself, he ungallantly complains to Aricia of being "ashamed and in despair" on its account[28] and "lost to reason in a raging tide."[29] Indeed, he avows it to her only because, as he puts it, "reason is yielding to violence" in him.[30] Later, in consideration of Phaedra's guilty passion as well as his own, he expostulates against "what love has done to poison all this house."[31] Like Phaedra, Aricia too is of a "guilty stem,"[32] and like Hippolytus, she too transgresses against her father's line and her own proud will to chastity when she returns Hippolytus's love. To complete this sorry erotic rundown of Racine's cast, Hippolytus has sworn off sex in the first place out of disgust over his father's "far-flung chain of amorous deceits"[33]: the last known links of that brazen chain were Theseus's desertion of Phaedra's sister and his abduction of Phaedra.

To put Racine's tragic setup back into focus, his play turns on Phaedra at center stage agonizing over her indomitable desire for her stepson while that stepson braces close by to elope with the daughter of an "odious house."[34] Reminders of Phaedra's blood taint of bestiality intermix early with tidings of Theseus off on some new exploit or dalliance. A false report of Theseus's death takes Phaedra off the incestuous-adulterous hook until Theseus's sudden return. Racine added that twist of Theseus's rumored death to Euripides' simpler plot line so as to ease the tormented heroine's wicked way to propositioning Hippolytus rather than just dying of shame as her finer instincts demand. More, on top of her gall at Hippolytus's rebuff of her, Racine gave Phaedra a new erotic motive, jealousy of Aricia, to help counteract her nagging scruples over Oenone's slander of Hippolytus that followed. And for good measure Racine threw in an embarrassingly phony, embarrassingly phallic frameup to help make that slander stick: Phaedra, rebuffed, draws Hippolytus's sword to run herself through if he holds off; Oenone intrudes to restrain Phaedra; Hippolytus rushes off without his sword—which Oenone can then claim that the lascivious lad had drawn on her resisting mistress in the heat of his passion. Oenone's slander sticks so fast that when Hippolytus, to defend himself against it without compromising Phaedra, confesses his love for Aricia, Theseus objects: "I see your game. / You play the criminal to clear your name."[35] The guilt trap was foolproof.

Racine's characters all come to grief from his Phaedra's folly, three of them fatally. Oenone, disgraced, drowns herself; Hippolytus's horses drag him to his death as they stampede away from a bullish monster (up from Euripides' mere bull); Phaedra, rather than hanging herself quietly offstage as in Euripides, takes a blood-chilling poison that leaves her just time enough to come clean before the whole court as if in a public confessional. But none of these mortal casualties of the evil in Phaedra's system suffers from it in dying so much as Phaedra herself suffers over it from bitter first to bitter last in her bootless craving for purity. As was the order of the day, Racine meant this tragic spectacle to be no less edifying than entertaining.[36] In this he failed, for its unmistakable moral is that sin is stronger than reason, duty, pride, and charity combined, so that the more those infected with sin fight it, the guiltier they feel without in the least lessening its hold on them or the havoc it wreaks—quite the contrary. This indeed is Racine's overtheme: that Phaedra's sin scores an easy win.

Still less edifying is Racine's undertheme, which extends that sin to all our hearts. Racine's theater is, I repeat, nothing if not universally symbolic with its lofty, depersonalized, exemplary characters, its uniform, simplified, regulated language, and its compact, concentrated action unfolding by strict rules as if from inner necessity. Racine's textual message here is already universal: that (barring divine grace, unavailable to pagan Phaedra) sin will triumph wherever it takes hold. But wherein is the sin that goes into Racine's text in *Phaedra* universal? We do not all lust after bulls or in-laws, philander by abduction and desertion, or woo last survivors of deadly enemy houses: those foibles cannot be stretched worldwide. Racine's classicistic trick in *Phaedra* is that through those few assorted rarities he denotes one vast commonplace. But this he does subtextually.

That commonplace is sexual love, alias "Venus with her clutches on her prey." What Racine in his preface calls "the passions" comes down in his play itself to that single, untender, rapacious passion. The disparate instances of guilty love in the play proper are like so many images of love's basic ferocity and pain. "I foul the air with incest and deceit"[37]: thus Phaedra agonizes—yet again and again she forgets the incest and deceit to state her trouble as love itself, period. To Oenone she complains: "I feel love's raging thirst."[38] Even the bestiality in her maternal heritage goes by that one generic name: "As love's thrall, / Into what vileness did my mother fall!"[39] Hippolytus likewise, after having long been love's "implacable foe,"[40] must bear "love's piercing arrow everywhere"[41]: *that* he loves, not *whom* he loves, is his deeper hurt. For Aricia, "pain" is a simple synonym of "love."[42] She too speaks disdainfully of "love's mad miseries"[43]; indeed, she prizes Hippolytus just because he has never "bowed beneath / Love's yoke."[44] Racine's preface claims with that selfsame ambiguity that his play showed up the "weaknesses begot by love" (and not by illicit love specifically) as "true weaknesses."[45]

Subtextually, then, love itself, and not its aberrations or abuses, is the villain of the piece. As in Euripides, so in Racine, that villain is a villainess. "How

Venus hates us!" exclaims Phaedra in consideration of her family's woes.[46] But in Euripides, Phaedra is that jealous goddess's innocent instrument to punish Hippolytus for scorning love in favor of the hunt, whereas Racine turned Euripides' jealous goddess into a universal demoness ravaging the whole human breed, hunters and nonhunters alike. As Racine's Phaedra tells it, at her first sight of Hippolytus "I knew myself possessed by Venus."[47] This was demonic possession with a vengeance.

That the guilty love in Racine's text is figurative of any and all love, that subtextually it spells love pure and simple, is highlighted in the text itself by that rumor of Theseus's death that Racine introduced into Euripides' plot as if to make this very point. With Theseus presumed dead, Phaedra's love for Hippolytus ceases to be guilty without changing in any other way. Most to the point, it does not stop feeling guilty: "I abhor myself still more than you despise me," she tells Hippolytus by way of declaring her love.[48] Then, with Theseus's sudden return, that selfsame, self-identical love turns guilty again. It follows like a flash of inner awareness that the guilty love is one with the guiltless love. No spectator or reader can miss this snap proof even if no spectator or reader takes special notice of it.

Racine's transformation of Venus into a universal scourge can be seen as a consequence of his giving Hippolytus that "weakness" of loving Aricia. For in so doing he deprived Venus of her grievance against an unloving Hippolytus, which in the Greek original was her sole ground for setting up Phaedra to frame the luckless lad. Racine's critics are right to point out that in the process he left Venus without even that shabby reason of her pique at Hippolytus for victimizing poor Phaedra as she does. But it is of the essence of Racine's Venus that she needs no special, personal reason to victimize us, male and female alike. So wanton was the fierce rut goddess fantasized by Racine that one suspects that he gave Phaedra her fair rival not, as he claimed, to provide Hippolytus with some foible or failing, which that demoted tragic hero no longer required, but because he could not conceive of Hippolytus resisting Phaedra's heated advances without an amorous alternative waiting for him in the wings.

Phaedra, unable to shake or propitiate her divine tormentor, "implacable Venus," supplicates her before knowing about Aricia: "Hippolytus flouts you . . . / Take vengeance, Goddess; our causes are the same. / Force him to love ."[49] This black mass might by rights have given the punitive goddess pause in the Greek original; in Racine's rewrite it comes too late, for there Hippolytus already loves by that point in the plot. Besides, in Racine's rewrite the goddess's cause is no longer love on pain of destruction, but destruction through love. More than just her deadly demonic pique shows through the beast raining "smoke and blood and flame" that destroys Hippolytus.[50] On the one symbolic side, that beast emerges from the waves as Venus herself did; on the other, it throws back to those lusty bulls in Phaedra's family tree. The jealous wrath that was the venereal goddess's in Euripides reappears in Racine as Phaedra's jealous fury on learning about her rival. All her earlier sufferings "were but foretastes of this agony," Phaedra then declares[51]—an agony that unmistakably comes of her passion itself and not its unlawfulness. "Aricia must die," she tells Oenone as a result, and again: "My murderous hands are itching to be stained / With innocent blood."[52]

But love, indeed sex, in *Phaedra* is not just a devastating, devouring, demeaning force; it is also a relentless fate. Fatedness is built into the very structure of Racine's theater with its tight-knit unity all in metronomic cadences and formularistic euphonies line by line. In *Phaedra*, that fatedness is also explicit. When Hippolytus wonders aloud whether he should brave his father's taboo of Aricia and "commit my youth to love's delirium," his governor responds: "Ah, Sir, if love's appointed hour has come, / It's vain to reason."[53] And to Phaedra fretting late along over the "dark, shameful crime" of adulterous incest that she, "alas," did not even commit, her nurse remarks: "You love. But who can conquer destiny? / Lured by a fatal spell, you were not free."[54] These two attendants in Racine's update double for the deleted Greek goddesses and chorus to affirm love's fatedness, leaving it for the principals themselves to express the guilt in their love. This illogical combination of fatedness and guilt in *Phaedra* resonates with the sense deep in all Christians, ex- and post-Christians inclusive, that sex, though natural, is naughty. Racine even identified sex with original sin in *Phaedra* through the motif of Phaedra's blood taint.

Textually, Thomas of Britain and Gottfried von Strassburg in their Tristan sagas already dealt in illicit love as generic love—as love *tout court*. Textually, they too already saw love as violating the social and moral order while ultimately destroying those most sorely smitten with it. But neither explicitly nor implicitly was love as such shameful, let alone sinful, for these two great rhyming romancers. It took Jansenism with its pious shudder at the flesh to culpabilize sexual love in and of itself for a Racine and his admiring public. Likely it is these Jansenist depths of *Phaedra* more than any exclusive Frenchness of its poetry that have confined its gut appeal to its native France as distinct from the majesty and magic it exudes equally abroad. For Jansenism died hard in French Catholicism even after being condemned by Rome in the first years of the eighteenth century. Meanwhile the Jansenist strain in French culture has if anything gained in strength detached from its Christian moorings, its primary lesson being that, as in *Phaedra*, there is no human way out of human depravity.

In Racine's text Phaedra's love is guilty. In his subtext all love is guilty. In his text Phaedra's conflict between deviant love and guilt drives her over the brink.

That guilt over her abnormal love is the same guilt writ large that his subtext posits as the normal wages of sexual love, however legitimate its object. Thus Racine illuminated the normal through the abnormal, or the mean through the extreme. So, oddly, did the late-nineteenth-century school of naturalism, otherwise the polar opposite of Racine's highly stylized poetic abstractions. Naturalism featured social pathology with the aim of showing it lurking within social normalcy, as when Ibsen used a degenerative family to show that the family as such is degenerative. Comparably, Racine dramatized overt sexual guilt so as to show up the covert guilt attaching to sexuality itself under the Christian dispensation. The crucial point of comparison is that in both cases the abnormal was textual and the normal subtextual. Only subtextually did Racine universalize and fundamentalize the indecency and destructiveness of Phaedra's lust. Textually Phaedra's monstrous love is out of line from first to last and exemplifies no more than the force of untrammeled evil. Even textually, though, the trammels on evil were illusory in *Phaedra*, just as subtextually all love, however unmonstrous, was of an evil kind with Racine's hapless heroine's. In sum, Racine's heartless Venus gave no quarter, and that no quarter was irresistible.

NOTES

1. Jean Racine, *Oeuvres complètes*, vol. 1, *Théâtre, Poésies* (Paris: Pléiade, 1950), 763. This volume is cited hereafter as Racine.

2. To be mythically exact, Neptune does his son Theseus's angry bidding in return for Theseus's having once cleared the river Styx of brigands.

3. Racine, 764.

4. In giving Hippolytus "quelque faiblesse" in the form of misdirected love, Racine may well have been following, not Aristotle directly, but Boileau's Aristotelian advice in *L'art poétique* (1674) to "give big hearts some weaknesses" ("aux grands coeurs donnez quelques faiblesses"). Beyond that, he shared Boileau's sense that love should "appear a weakness and not a virtue." (Actually, Hippolytus's priggishness in Euripides was already more of a weakness than was even Hippolytus's tabooed love in Racine.)

5. Racine, 765.

6. "It suffices to judge well in order to do well": René Descartes, *Discours de la méthode*, part 3, in *Oeuvres et lettres* (Paris: Pléiade, 1958), 144.

7. Racine, 773; Jean Racine, *Phaedra*, trans. Richard Wilbur (San Diego: Harcourt Brace Jovanovich, 1986), 18. I shall use this faithful poetic rendition, cited hereafter as Wilbur, except where a more literal equivalence is needed.

8. Racine, 792; Wilbur, 54.

9. Racine, 776.

10. Ibid., 788.

11. Ibid., 789.

12. Ibid., 809; Wilbur, 83.
13. Racine, 792.
14. Ibid., 820; Wilbur, 104.
15. Racine, 792.
16. Ibid., 777.
17. Ibid., 790.
18. Ibid., 777.
19. Ibid., 775.
20. Ibid., 768; Wilbur, 10.
21. Racine, 776; Wilbur, 23.
22. Racine, 805.
23. Ibid., 820; Wilbur, 104.
24. Racine, 793; Wilbur, 56.
25. Racine, 768; Wilbur, 11.
26. Racine, 771; Wilbur, 14.
27. Racine, 770.
28. Ibid., 785; Wilbur, 39.
29. Racine, 784; Wilbur, 39.
30. Racine, 784.
31. Ibid.; Wilbur, 66.
32. Racine, 770; Wilbur, 13.
33. Racine, 769; Wilbur, 12.
34. Racine, 809; Wilbur, 83 (literally, "odious blood").
35. Racine, 804; Wilbur, 74.
36. Racine, 765.
37. Ibid., 809; Wilbur, 83.
38. Racine, 776; Wilbur, 22.
39. Racine, 775; Wilbur, 21.
40. Racine, 769. Further, "love's enemy": ibid., 784; Wilbur, 38.
41. Racine, 785; Wilbur, 39.
42. Racine, 782.
43. Ibid., 781.
44. Ibid., 782; Wilbur, 34.
45. Racine, 765; Wilbur, 5.
46. Racine, 775; Wilbur, 21.
47. Racine, 776; Wilbur, 23.
48. Racine, 789.
49. Ibid., 794; Wilbur, 57.
50. Racine, 817; Wilbur, 101.
51. Racine, 808; Wilbur, 82.
52. Racine, 809; Wilbur, 83.
53. Racine, 770; Wilbur, 13.
54. Racine, 810; Wilbur, 84.

8

A Wanderer on Earth
Goethe's *The Sorrows of Young Werther*

In a letter of June 1774 young Johann Wolfgang Goethe announced a novel by him then going to press "in which I depict a young man endowed with deep, pure feeling and true insight who loses himself in rapturous dreams and wears himself out with idle speculation until at length, unnerved to boot by hapless passions, especially an issueless love, he puts a bullet through his head."[1] This abstract of *The Sorrows of Young Werther* by its author himself is strikingly lopsided in that the issueless love cited only last, addendumlike, among his hero's fatal troubles is far and away the most conspicuous one of the lot in the novel itself. The second most conspicuous, a falling out by young Werther with high society in a southern German capital, even goes wholly unmentioned in the expectant author's summary of his plot. Young Werther does dream rapturously, as that forecast of the novel states. On the other hand, the sorry youngster hardly speculates, let alone wears himself out in the process. As for his unnerving "hapless passions," the work itself divulges a single one: that selfsame issueless love that Goethe's advance synopsis mentions in a mere appendage to an afterthought. Can the author have been ambivalent about his luckless hero's fatal love?

When young Werther's tragic sorrows hit the Frankfurt book fair that autumn of 1774, they swept Europe overnight like a contagion. Goethe's epistolary novel containing them was styled as a sympathetic editor's painstaking documentation and reconstruction of a gifted youth's tragic course from seeming *joie de vivre* to suicide: twenty-odd months of letters by Werther, mostly to a nondescript friend named Wilhelm, topped off by the editor's chilling account of Werther's last days, itself incorporating additional letters as well as some notations and fragments. This correspondence with Wilhelm takes off from a liberating flight by Werther from his hometown to a backwater village, Wahlheim ("chosen home"), in search of an outer and inner retreat for his tender soul and budding genius. A would-be artist, Werther tries sketching the lush local landscape, but he exults in it all too extravagantly even to get started. So he contents himself instead with reveling in the rustic scenes round about him and, between times, thrilling to Homer in the Greek original. Then one day he espies lovely Lotte cutting bread for her six siblings in her charge and is instantly, convulsively, irremediably smitten: thenceforth, as he puts it, "the whole world is lost around me"[2] except only adorable, adored Lotte. Underneath Werther's exalted fancy, Lotte keeps house for her widowed father, a bailiff, and is betrothed to decent, dull Albert, whom she duly marries some thirty letters later even after she has grown all too close to Werther sentimentally on the side.

By then Werther, lovesick, has fled the newlyweds' vicinity and entered state service at a legation in a distant town, half hoping to forget his Lotte now lost to him. For six months he holds out against all his inclinations amidst the petty, rule-bound, mannered official set until he once inadvertently breaches the snobbish decorum of the local upper social crust. Ugly tongue wagging follows, prompting his resignation. He next visits a friendly prince's estate, but after a single month there he can shun his fate no longer and returns to Wahlheim to mope in Lotte's shadow, estranged from everyone and everything else. When, on Albert's insistence, Lotte eventually tries to hold him at bay, he abandons all hope. Gloomily he starts penning a suicide letter to Lotte, but desists briefly to pay her a forbidden evening visit in Albert's absence at which he reads to her from his own translation of the ancient Gaelic bard Ossian (actually Goethe's of an enchanting fake by James Macpherson, exposed only later). This mournful recitation so carries her away that she yields momentarily to his inflamed kisses. He staggers home in a daze and, after a long sleep, resumes his farewell message to her on a lyrical high, confident that she will be his alone in the next world. He completes it newly elated after having sent for the loan of Albert's pistols and received them through his servant from Lotte's very own trembling hands. Even so, the misfire artist, functionary, and lover bungles his carefully planned supreme act in its turn, with the result that he agonizes twelve hours before breathing his last.

On an uncritical reading, Goethe's Werther dies of an unrequited love that has brought on a radical alienation from life. But the fictive editor of *Werther* intimates, and Werther's earliest letters themselves already disclose, what Goethe spelled out in that private announcement of his novel quoted earlier: that the drastic course of Werther's all-consuming love for Lotte, perhaps even his choice of a beloved beyond his reach in the first place (as Lotte herself once suggests to him), came of the deep-lying maladjustment to life of an ineffectual dreamer more to be pitied than admired, let alone emulated. In 1775, reacting against the suicidal Werther craze that his book touched off, Goethe prefaced a reprint of it with some doggerel ending:

> You lament, you love him, oh dear soul,
> And rescue from disgrace his memory.
> Look, his spirit signals you from hell:
> *Be a man, and do not follow me.*[3]

Beginning in 1782, he revised the book for a second edition, published in 1787, meant to lend it more the stamp of a pathological case history. In this reworking he radicalized Werther's ultimate antagonism to the world at large excepting only Lotte. To do so he increased by a good third the pretended editor's terminal section with its now still more detached, almost clinical tone even in its (incongruous) recording of Werther's private thoughts and feelings. Above all, where the original edition already reflected on the hero through others in passing—once through his felt kinship with a loved-and-left girl who drowns herself, and again through the bailiff's clerk gone mad for hopeless love of the bailiff's daughter, namely Lotte—the new version worked a sharper, finer, deeper mirroring into the action. A farmhand covets a widow; her brother drives him hence; he murders a luckier successor—and Werther, who has fantasized murdering Albert, identifies with the murderer as an impassioned odd man out. He considers the poor wretch "guiltless even as a criminal" and desperately pleads his cause to the bailiff and the bailiff's standby, Albert. But they, not Werther, are in the right. More, Werther knows it, "yet he felt as though he would have to renounce his innermost being if he avowed it, if he admitted it." He slinks off in deep distress after the bailiff tells him over and over with finality about the pitiable culprit: "No, there is no help for him!" A note later found in Werther's papers reads: "There is no help for you, poor wretch! I see plainly that there is no help for us."

Taken together, these textual revisions of the 1780s should have cast a more critical light on Werther by distancing readers from him at a longer stretch just before his suicide and by bringing out the solidarity he felt with crime against his own better judgment. Yet despite Goethe's ostensible purpose, the second edition of the novel is if anything more partial to Werther on balance than the first. Its love triangle is more nearly equilateral in that Goethe upped the signs of Lotte's ill-controlled return affection for her ardent soul's mate to the detriment of her philistine spouse vouchsafing her a mere budgeted bland fondness. As a result, the amplified editorial account of Werther's last days, with its closer neutral look at the now-tightened existential bind on him, actually raises his moral stature. Similarly, in point of dignity his deliberate self-sacrifice has it all over his depressive defeat in the first edition. So does this retreat into suicide now show to advantage as set off against the farmhand's descent into murder. Clearly Goethe was torn both ways between censuring and vindicating Werther.

Just as clearly the source of Goethe's ambivalence toward Werther was one with the personal origins of his novel about the sad lad. Young Werther's frustrated romance with betrothed, then wedded, Lotte was young Goethe's own frustrated romance with a betrothed, then wedded, flesh-and-blood small-town Lotte, Charlotte Buff, in almost every material particular short of Werther's suicide itself: at the real-life danger point Goethe fled the real-life young couple's proximity instead. Eerily, only weeks after this flight in lovelorn sorrow from his actual Lotte, the very suicide that Goethe had been contemplating in her tiny town of Wetzlar was committed there by a young acquaintance of his—a disenchanted underling at a legation, Carl Wilhelm Jerusalem, ill used by official society and hopelessly in love with a legation colleague's wife. Goethe, deeply affected, obtained from his real Lotte's husband, Johann Christian Kestner, himself likewise a junior official at a legation, a full account of Jerusalem's last deed and evidently experienced it as his own by proxy, flubbed gunshot and all. Fictive young Werther incubated for some eighteen months afterwards, then emerged from Goethe's pen as his twin both outwardly and inwardly even to the extent of sharing his birthday, but with young Jerusalem's tragic fate as his Lotte-less lot. Real Lotte of Wetzlar showed through her homonymic fictional counterpart in Wahlheim almost intact. But at Goethe's hands her real husband, Kestner, came across narrower and pettier as Albert, recast more in the mold of the legation milieu in Wetzlar that was Kestner's in real life and had been Jerusalem's and indeed Goethe's as well. Wronged Kestner complained kindly to Goethe, who later made shabby amends in the reworked version. Because that propriety-minded husband had feared gossip about Goethe and Lotte when he saw the original novel on its way into print, the reedited Albert fears gossip about Werther and Lotte: tit for tat. Kestner had neither claimed nor received credit when his dispassionate, affecting account to Goethe of Jerusalem's suicide fed into the fictive editor's report in *Werther* on the hero's last days, with even some whole sentences by Kestner transcribed almost word for word. As this appropriation shows, that all-knowing editor in *Werther*, nominally the author's mouthpiece, derived from the same prototype as fictive Lotte's insipid spouse.[4]

But Goethe's ambivalence toward Kestner alias Albert was as nothing beside his ambivalence toward his own alter ego, Werther. Even as he revised *Werther* in the 1780s, he was secretly involved with another married Lotte, Charlotte von Stein, so that its emotional substratum, a fixture of his inner world since 1774, was again actual for him in the process: he was as if back in Wetzlar hating his own helpless love. In the revision his fertile ambivalence toward his sorrowful hero shows in sharpest relief as mirrored through Werther's self-identified farmhand who murders a lucky rival as Werther himself only dreams of doing. As already noted, Goethe added this farmhand episode to disassociate himself the more emphatically from his Werther, now self-identified with a criminal. Yet a Werther self-identified with a farmhand who commits his fantasized murder for him once removed throws right back to Goethe self-identified with a Werther, or indeed with a Jerusalem, who had committed his fantasized suicide for him once removed. Here, then, was the matrix of the device that Goethe himself later called "mirroring" and that shaped the whole of his next novel, *Wilhelm Meister's Apprenticeship*: the farmhand's experience reflected Werther's exactly as Werther's reflected Goethe's own.

Goethe nursed his ambivalence toward Werther and *Werther* his whole life long. While preparing his second edition, he told his second Lotte, with tongue not quite in cheek, that "the editor was wrong not to have shot himself once his job was done."[5] In the 1790s he projected a third edition intended to incorporate new, serene letters by Werther from Switzerland to be derived from his own letters of 1779 to his new Lotte. Repeatedly, meanwhile, he repudiated the novel as mere therapy for his youthful morbid self-dramatization and his then-fashionable revulsion against being sensible. In his middle years, until his autobiography of 1814 inclusive, he preferred to blame *Werther* on a "disgust with life" rampant in his generation that he professedly wrote out of his system through Werther's suicide; in neither version of the novel, however, does any such "disgust with life" play a part. In a further turnabout he wondered on rereading *Werther* in 1816 how he could ever have endured forty more years of Werther's absurd world after he wrote it.[6] He told Johann Peter Eckermann (his Boswell) in 1824 that he was afraid of *Werther* because of the personal pathology behind it; reminded by Eckermann that he had officially blamed Werther's sorrows on the Zeitgeist, he snapped back that no, he had been wrong, he had "lived, loved, and deeply suffered! That was it."[7] That same year he backed up this resurgence of his Lotte pathos with a couplet "To Werther" assuring his cut-off other self that he ("you") had not missed much by quitting young. But then he still could veer right around again in old age and dismiss his whole Wetzlar or Lotte experience as "of no great account."[8]

Constant in Goethe's unstable attitude toward Werther over the years was the tension between his damning judgment of the anguished youth and his gut partiality to him. Both came of his sickness unto death from a love of Lotte that survived in full fury deep inside him. Or rather, both came of his sickness not quite unto death,[9] so that through *Werther* he argued against his envy of the suicide committed by Jerusalem, Lotte's townsman stuck in an amorous rut like his own: this "like" was the real-life mother of all his "mirrorings." His tension between denying and affirming Werther, never resolved, informs both versions of *Werther* equally in their dialectic of text and subtext—of Werther suffering because he is wrong as against Werther suffering because he is right.

In *Werther* the editor's is the chief formal frown at the principles its hero upholds and at the course he pursues. Unlike the usual didactic narrator of Goethe's day, the editor in *Werther* refrains from overt sermonizing. He thereby makes Goethe's point only the more effectively as he pays nonjudgmental last respects to a great soul gone astray beyond recall. Before Werther reaches that point of no return, his close associates each and all speak out at one point or another to warn him against himself in the mode of tolerant civility, sweet reasonableness, and solicitous concern. Such futile warnings are issued by his correspondent Wilhelm and, through Wilhelm, his mother (as reflected in his replies to Wilhelm); by Albert, by Lotte's father, and even by Lotte herself; indeed, often enough by Werther himself concessively in his epistolary monologues or, later, in his private second thoughts as recorded by the all-knowing editor. The cumulative effect of these unheeded admonitions is of a Werther demanding compliance, and compliance alone, from the world at large; respecting or even acknowledging others only insofar as their spirits resonate with his; averse to all moderation or restraint, all rules or limits, of whatever kind; pushing passion, namely his own, against a tutelary, monitory resistance within his circle and even his own psyche, its maxims the more offensive to him for being obviously sane and humane. To an uncomprehending Albert he declares excitedly for "Passion! Drunkenness! Madness!" in the name of "all exceptional people who ever accomplished anything great, anything seemingly impossible." Carried away by his own rhetoric, he cries: "You stand there so complacent, so detached, you proper lot," then concludes that "the modicum of sense one may have counts for little or nothing when passion rages."[10] His defense of the homicidal farmhand as having acted out of pure passion falls on still-deafer ears than this earlier pitch for passion in the abstract: the bailiff, "quite understandably" unmoved, silences him with the compelling objection "that on those terms all law would be voided, all public security destroyed," and Werther, while acquiescing inwardly in the bailiff's rejoinder, takes it as aimed at him personally when Albert chimes in with the bailiff. Even before he meets Lotte, his letters document his self-coddling ("I treat my poor heart like a sick child, granting its every wish"[11]), his manic moodiness (or frequent swings "from grief to exuberance, from sweet melancholy to pernicious passion"[12]), and his pathetic self-aggrandizing ("to be misunderstood is the fate of my kind"[13]). Once he falls for Lotte he acknowledges his sickness, but on that single amorous score. To Wilhelm, who tells him to forget Lotte if he cannot have her, he pleads helplessness and likens himself to "an unfortunate gradually succumbing to an incurable creeping disease."[14] One of his next outpourings begins: "True, if my sickness could be cured."[15] Lotte, though, applies the term without restriction when she tells him toward the last: "Werther, you are very sick."[16] Conflicted Lotte aside, Werther finds no fellowship in his emotional extravagance, with three telltale exceptions: one suicide, one madman, and one killer.

Thus Werther is virtually isolated in his titular sorrows and finally as if quarantined by right reason, his own right reason inclusive. Yet the cause of good sense loses out not just in him, but in the novel about him, for all the author's contrary intentions. One reason is that, as Goethe's lyrical strain personified, Werther is possessed of a compelling force of sentiment and expression that easily defeats his author's cautionary purpose. More, the cards are stacked on Werther's side of his quarrel with existence in that the bulk of the novel consists of his own powerful words. For the rest, the editorial report at the end, besides quoting him lengthily, is still largely cast in his own perspective. Its style is antidotal in its sobriety perhaps, but that sobriety is no match for the ultimate argument of his gripping suicide that it conveys. Yet none of these advantages would avail Werther much on his suicidal side of the clash of purposes and values within the work were it not that his outlook and behavior carry some conviction in their own right.

This they do despite the risk they also carry. Werther comes to Wahlheim seeking refuge from city life and personal entanglements, from constriction and artificiality: "How happy I am to be gone!" is his inauspicious opening line.[17] He would lose himself in all of nature there, and to the last he aspires to the "fullness of the infinite" as against "dull, cold consciousness."[18] At the same time, except in observing simple country folk, as was then the fine fashion, he prefers his inner world to human society. Society hems him in, whereas nature empowers him—or so he feels. So far, so unproblematic, until he falls in love and, seeking a corrective, ventures on a career. In both cases he enters upon a collision course with reality, given the absolute primacy he accords to the heart over the head, to vision over refractory fact (read: *his* heart, *his* vision). He comes out of himself and the garden of nature only to focus on Lotte exclusively, to covet her uncompromisingly. Not that he fashions her arbitrarily into an unattainable ideal by dint of a prior vocation for sorrow: he does love her as personally and accurately as love permits—and desperately. This last is his fatal virtue: he makes of his love a life-and-death imperative, in pointed contrast to Albert husbanding his seemly conjugal affection as domestic decorum dictates. In Werther's desperation over Lotte, nature turns in his estimate from a feast of perpetual creation into a monster devouring its own creatures. At the same time he reverts from an exalted selfless cult of all-enfolding nature to a Christian faith in personal survival, with the result that he feels himself to be existing here below only on time off from eternity, as "a wanderer on earth."[19] Death therewith goes for him from an unfocused to a focused ecstasy—from a supreme communion with the elements to an erotic union with Lotte. First he declares with scriptural overtones in his suicide note to Lotte: "I sacrifice myself for you," but after they have kissed he adds: "I fly to meet you and enfold you and remain at your side in an eternal embrace in the sight of the infinite." Clearly he does not belong here below. But is the fault his (text) or the world's (subtext)?

Nowhere is the fault more the world's than at the legation he quits after he innocently lingers on at a reception beyond the point at which untitled guests are no longer welcome. His host nudges him graciously, he bows out smiling, well and good, only the next thing he knows, the whole town is talking. In the original *Werther* this putdown, based on a real one suffered by Jerusalem, turns Werther away from practical, worldly endeavor once and for all, in effect from this-worldly life itself. But in the revised version it weighs into the action after the fact only as one of the many pieces of earthly unpleasantness that the hero recollects as he opts for death. The change was in order. Werther is by temperament unfit for his chosen career, or for any other, from the first. He is close to the breaking point on the job well before that scandal strikes. The punctilious, mindless narrowness required for routinized paper pushing in concert, or competition, with aspiring junior officials at a snobbish petty court turns him off in no time, what with his craving for boundless self-expression and self-expansion. As Goethe afterwards insisted, this vain and vapid craving was modish among the self-styled superior misfits of his generation, like the waistcoat and trousers that Werther wears or (in the first edition) the folksy diction that he affects. It was no simple corollary of the bourgeois ideal of freedom then on its triumphant rise in Europe, as with Marxist myopia it is commonly perceived to have been. In any case, even first-edition Werther dies not of his professional failure, but—like a Phaedra or a Tristan before him—of an unquenchable forbidden love to which he was predisposed from the start. Nor is he even on the make professionally in joining the legation; he is just trying, albeit halfheartedly, to get over his off-limits Lotte. Not Goethe's Werther but Werther's remote descendant, Stendhal's Julien Sorel, joins battle with the social order, and at that not even upstart Julien's heart is really in it, as he discovers too late (and as the next chapter will show). Unlike Goethe's later Wilhelm Meister, his Werther is no more class-specific than the private means he needs to nurse his sorrows—even if Goethe did later call him, among other misnomers, a typical bourgeois of the time.

In brief, young Werther is set up from the outset to suffer in close, sustained human intercourse of whatever kind, and to suffer beyond endurance from his love of an unattainable Lotte. Goethe does not even hint how Werther got that vulnerable way; his *Werther* is not yet the *Bildungsroman* he invented next, let alone a precocious Freudian psychogram.[20] In fact, for all Werther's intimate soul-searching, Goethe did not individualize him much. Granted, Goethe told it straight in old age when he avowed that it was his first Lotte herself after all, and no fashionable "disgust with life," that had brought him close to his own suicide and then to Werther's suicide instead. Werther was no less a child of the century, his sorrows no less a *mal de siècle*, or at all odds a cultural malady rampant in the Germanies of the 1770s as also elsewhere in Europe. *Werther*, Goethe's failed attempt to purge himself of his Lotte ailment, was at the same time an object lesson in sickly egoism writ large. When the object went over bigger than the lesson, Goethe revised the text to underscore its intended warning as best he could while still respecting Werther's story as originally set forth by him in the guise of documented fact.

That intended warning was Goethe's overt message, to wit, that Werther's exquisite sensibility, his absolute demands on life, his sky-high premium on passion, are so much poison. But that message carried the covert questions whether great souls really can cut themselves down to size, whether survival should be their defining value anyhow, even whether suicide is of necessity self-destructive. The whole of Werther's worthy being (which is what his name means) is inimical to the whole of existence outside of his own self, whether to transitory terms of existence such as a civil, a social, a moral order or to fixed facts of existence such as seasons passing or visions fading. Goethe came out against Werther in the text of the novel while in its subtext he too, like his hero, rejected reality itself, or opted out.

Werther is to my knowledge unique among literary classics in its bottom-heavy imbalance between text and subtext. Their interrelation being an am-bivalent one, the text might be expected to keep the subtext under wraps, the way our preferred thoughts or feelings drive our counter thoughts and feelings into hiding. But not only does the subtext overwhelm the text in impact even after Goethe's revision of the 1780s that was expressly intended to redress the balance; it is on the same level of explicitness as the text, being conveyed not indirectly by hints or symbols or implications, but eloquently in so many words through the author's apparent mouthpiece, and indeed in many more words than the embattled text itself. The storm and stress of this ambivalence, with its repudiating and its repudiated thrust fighting it out in the open, projects such a powerful, intimate authorial presence that, unlike Goethe's later works, *Werther* can hardly be read without the figure of its author himself hovering over it, equally unable to accept or to reject life without Lotte once and for all. The result of this acute dilemma was a baffling, troubling, haunting novel that catapulted Goethe to lasting glory and dogged him like a nemesis right into his Olympian old age.

NOTES

1. Goethe to Gottlob Friedrich Ernst Schönborn, 1 June 1774, in Erich Trunz, ed., *Goethes Werke*, vol. 6, *Quellen und Daten zur Geschichte des "Werther"-Romans* (Hamburg: Wegner, 1968), 521.

2. 19 June 1771. References to *Werther* are by letter date; unreferenced quotations are from the editor's narrative at the end.

3. Quoted by Trunz, 528; Kurt Rothmann, *Erläuterungen und Dokumente, Johann Wolfgang Goethe: Die Leiden des jungen Werthers* (Stuttgart: Reclam, 1987), 70: "Du beweinst, du liebst ihn, liebe Seele, / Rettest sein Gedächtniss von der Schmach; / Sieh, dir winkt sein Geist aus seiner Hölle: / *Sei ein Mann, und folge mir nicht nach.*"

4. A further, lesser personal source for *Werther* was a mother and daughter, Sophie and Maximiliane von La Roche, whom Goethe visited on his flight from Lotte. An autobiographic epistolary novel by the mother was a suggestive precedent for *Werther* at least as to form, while the daughter's dark eyes and her jealous husband-to-be rubbed off onto Lotte and Albert respectively.

5. Goethe to Charlotte von Stein, 25 June 1786, in *Goethes Briefe an Frau von Stein* (Stuttgart: Cotta, 1905), 3:184.

6. Goethe to Karl Friedrich Zelter, 26 March 1816, in Trunz, 534.

7. Johann Peter Eckermann, *Gespräche mit Goethe* (Wiesbaden: Insel, 1955), 489–90 (conversation of 2 January 1824).

8. Quoted by Alfred Ehrentreich, "An der Peripherie von Goethes 'Werther,' " *Goethe Jahrbuch*, 100 (1983): 270.

9. A neglected reference for Goethe's *suicide manqué* over Lotte is his letter of 1774 to piqued Kestner: "If I am still alive it's you I owe it to, so you aren't Albert." Quoted ibid., 267.

10. 12 August [1771].
11. 13 May [1771].
12. Ibid.
13. 17 May [1771].
14. 8 August [1771].
15. 28 August [1771].
16. 4 December [1771].
17. 4 May [1771].
18. 16 December [1772].
19. 16 June [1772].

20. But Werther's love at first sight for someone else's woman playing mother beside her widowed father is a Freudian giveaway. (Goethe's second Lotte, incidentally, was seven years his senior and a seven-time mother.)

9

On Death Row
Stendhal's *The Red and the Black*

By common consent, *The Red and the Black* of 1830 is not just a great, but a very romantic, novel. What is romantic about it is above all its hero, Julien Sorel, whom it characterizes as "the very type of the unhappy man at war with all of society."[1] Less purely romantic is its author, Stendhal, who often, like an old-style *moraliste*, shakes a censorious finger at Julien for passing happiness by while waging a full-time, feverish campaign of social climbing.

Stendhal's romantic Julien, a small-town French woodcutter's son bullied at home for his bookish bent, sets out with teeth clenched to scale the heights of a society that he abominates with good cause. This society is that of Restoration France toward 1830 dominated by a multilayered old nobility, a newer imperial nobility, a powerful *bourgeoisie d'affaires* aping and threatening both these aristocratic orders, and a tangled, tenuous network of power brokerage in the service of throne and altar extending to even the remotest and lowliest of provincial offices. Julien has a secret, subversive cult of titanic Napoleon. Under the defunct empire, he tells himself, he would have won glory fairly and squarely by serving his idol in a red uniform of battle; now instead, making do under the empire's inglorious successor regime, he learns the Vulgate by heart, feigns piety, and dons a black cassock, with his sights sullenly set on a bishop's miter.

Except, though, for a term he spends in a provincial seminary failing to learn humility, Julien's career is worldly. First he tutors a local mayor's children and seduces the mayor's wife, Madame de Rênal. Later he serves a marquis in Paris as secretary until he gets the daughter of the house, Mathilde, pregnant. A penitent Madame de Rênal writes to the marquis denouncing Julien as a base seducer just as the triumphant upstart is being fitted out with a fake noble lineage qualifying him to marry Mathilde. Infuriated, Julien shoots Madame de Rênal, a capital crime by the books despite her prompt recovery. Afterwards, facing the gallows, he realizes that even on his own duplicitous terms he had been living falsely before—that at bottom his career had meant nothing to him and Madame de Rênal everything. She on her side, repenting of her repentance, returns to his arms in his death cell. She dies of sorrow when he is guillotined while crazed Mathilde lavishly enshrines his head in a grotto.

The romantic hero was not typically a careerist like Julien. But he was typically at odds with extant society while at the same time yearning for inclusion, for acceptance, for belonging. Along with fictive Werther, it was a celebrated character out of nonfiction, Jean-Jacques Rousseau, who set this conflicted style before romanticism enveloped Europe. One form it took under romanticism was alienation in the very thick of society—assuming a society's coloration with an animus against it, as did Julien. Another was to scrutinize society's innermost workings with conspicuous distaste, as did Julien's author. *The Red and the Black*, subtitled *A Chronicle of 1830*, was, for a single novel, the late romantic ultimate in broad social sweep and close social observation.

In reaction against the abstract universalism of his bugbear, Racine, Stendhal meant the complex interplay of character and circumstance in *The Red and the Black* to derive from the dynamics of richly varied, rapidly shifting manners and morals, interests and attitudes, mindsets and sentiments, specific to the France of his time. Romanticism had already developed just such specificity about past eras, especially the Middle Ages; with *The Red and the Black* Stendhal brought this fictional historicism up to date. Balzac followed Stendhal's lead on a larger scale in *The Human Comedy*, but few single volumes of this interminable novelistic series (perhaps only *Eugénie Grandet, Old Goriot,* and *Lost Illusions*) can even compete with *The Red and the Black* for coverage of the social landscape of France in the protracted aftermath of the great Revolution. Further, where Stendhal recorded class traits with a deft touch, Balzac stylized and even overdrew them for dramatic effect. Stendhal, a drifter with no fixed political or other location, took an astute onlooker's wry delight in noting the ways of envy, vanity, and snobbery, of nervous grasping, fatuous fawning, and solemn cant, proper to the rule of priests and notables in a Restoration tottering to its close. Balzac for his part, a naïve royalist nostalgic for the devout, stable, serene old France that never was, worked out of, without ever working off, a rapt horror at the morbid unrest and infernal turmoil spawned, as he saw it, by that huge historic mistake dated 1789.

But no romantic, real or imaginary, topped Julien Sorel in his first manner, meaning Julien Sorel before his climactic pistol shots at Madame de Rênal, in prepossession with and estrangement from the social world around him. While Julien is on the make, he hates his social inferiors or equals for reminding him of his own lowly status even as he hates his social superiors for seeming to despise him. His sex life, above all, is social pathology pure. Initially he detests lovely Madame de Rênal just because of her loveliness, which perturbs his scheming ambition. Having resolved to seduce her as the proper thing for a would-be *galant homme* to do, "he sized her up like an enemy."[2] Clumsily he conquers that enemy, whereupon in his anxiety to play the seducer with aplomb he does not even enjoy his conquest. Love comes with time, but poisoned at its source—as "the joy of possessing, poor despised underling that he was, a woman so noble and so beautiful."[3] Long months afterwards, in the marquis's stuffy establishment and wearisome service, he muses while recollecting his provincial beginnings: "My fancies about Paris prevented me from appreciating such a sublime woman"[4]—this just as, upward bound, he resolves next to seduce the marquis's daughter, Mathilde. Proud Mathilde declares her love, and his vanity alone exults. She invites him to her room, and he suspects a trap. He goes defiantly, for several calculating reasons and only lastly because she is pretty. He performs lovelessly, she with shame and distaste: "Without suspecting it, they were motivated toward each other by feelings of intensest hate."[5] But in its aftermath their cold tryst flames red-hot in his memory. She brushes him off, and his passion soars. He wins her back by courting a rival; not the lover, though, but the *arriviste* gloats as he accedes through her womb to a noble title and a commission in the hussars.

Then he blows it—and reflects in jail about his intended victim, Madame de Rênal, even before his loving reunion with her: "Strange! I thought that by her letter to the marquis she had destroyed my future happiness forever, and less than a fortnight later I no longer care in the least about anything that concerned me then."[6] A surefire casualty of his pistol shots that had missed their mark, and of his total emotional turnabout that followed, was Mathilde. Facing the gallows, he feels Mathilde's fevered love as a nuisance, while her extravagant desperation on his account only irks him. But at the same time he also wonders concerning her: might he be unkind? "The question would have given him little pause when he was ambitious; the only shame in his eyes at that time was not to get ahead."[7]

Until his capital crime Julien is a reluctant hypocrite, acting out of professed sentiments he finds repugnant, in a frenetic campaign to crash a high society he despises as factitious, stifling, and—except in defending the shabby, shaky privileges it has retrieved from the refuse heap of unequal rights left behind by the Revolution—unprincipled. "I loved truth . . . ," he later reflects. "Where is it? . . . Everywhere hypocrisy, or at all odds fakery."[8] So far, so romantic. But after his capital crime Julien strikes out beyond the consecrated romantic range to recognize that previously, while on his own course of conscious hypocrisy and fakery, he had lost touch with his true feelings, stifled his humanity, and wound up putting Madame de Rênal's and his own life on the line for the sake of the mundane, meretricious values of the very society he so heartily despised. The falsity to himself at the heart of Julien's *arriviste* hypocrisy comes as no news to the reader after having been the running theme of authorial asides all through the narrative. But Julien's own self-disclosure, his recognition in extremis of his earlier falsity to himself, clinches it like proof positive, thereby turning the textual message of *The Red and the Black* from the vindication of the superior misfit, a romantic commonplace inspired by *Werther* and Rousseau, to a disclosure of the vanity of a life's purposes and strivings as seen from the vantage point of death row. Julien, the outsider to French society in 1830, self-made and then self-unmade, can read his own heart straight in the end only as an outsider to life itself for whom its fugitive joys are now so many hangman's meals—or, still more literally, so many love feasts with Madame de Rênal on his jailer's paid sufferance. Early in his deathwatch, before the love feasts begin, Julien already discovers to his surprise that the gallows perspective on joy boosts it sky-high instead of spoiling it. As he puts it: "I have known the art of enjoying life only since I have seen its end so close upon me."[9] Madame de Rênal's visits come later, as a bonus. "I would have died without knowing happiness had you not come to see me in this prison," he tells her[10]: here his last three words are crucial.

For all that, it is too late for truth or happiness beyond such fleeting glimpses of his loss. "The influence of my contemporaries wins out," Julien declaims in solitude; "speaking alone with myself, two steps away from death, I am still hypocritical."[11] Again, laughing like Mephistopheles: "1. I am a hypocrite as if someone were there listening to me. 2. I forget to live and love, though so few days are left to me . . ."[12]

Has Julien's self-disclosure in a death cell any wider human significance? Does it bring his fate—exceptional in the highest degree, and exactingly situated in his particular time and place—any closer to ours? Yes and again yes, provided only that Stendhal's subtext is brought in. This subtext has a rich prehistory and posthistory, with Stendhal's novel a milestone in between.

It is crucial to this subtext that Julien commits no real capital crime even if he does continually declare himself guilty of one. His crime qualifies as murder only by dint of a statutory anomaly: here Stendhal departed pointedly from the actual murder in the real court case on which his novel was based. It reduces Julien's criminal liability, moreover, that he enters into a trance, or "state of . . . semi-madness,"[13] on reading Madame de Rênal's letter to the marquis and reemerges only well after his attempted murder, when he learns of the victim's survival. Then too, for good measure, he provokes the biased bourgeois jury by calling it just that. In sum, he incurs a death sentence that comes across, by Stendhal's design, as undeserved.

Now for a digression that is none. In the Christian tradition human mortality was itself a capital punishment for Adam's sin, one no less in force even after Christ brought humans the prospect of salvation through divine grace. The punitive character of human mortality was common parlance throughout the Christian era; as the first modern tragic hero put it to himself, "What art thou, Faustus, but a man condemned to die?"[14] Most expressively, Pascal in two of his *pensées* likened the human lot to death row. "Imagine a number of men in chains, all sentenced to death, some of whom are slaughtered every day in full view of the others; those who remain see their own situation in that of their fellows and, eyeing one another with anguish and without hope, await their turn. This is the image of the human condition." Then again, in a specifically Christian variant: "A man in a cell, not knowing if sentence has been passed on him, having only an hour left to find out, and this hour being time enough to get it revoked if he knows it has been passed: it is unnatural for him to spend the hour not in finding out if that sentence has been passed, but in playing piquet."[15] Victor Hugo, in a novel of 1823 about an attempted "judicial murder" in early modern Iceland, remotely echoed the first of these two arresting *pensées*: "Being all condemned to death with indefinite stays of execution, we are morbidly curious about the poor fellow who knows at just what hour his stay of execution will be suspended."[16] Hugo's innocent Icelandic baron escapes the noose in the end; not so, however, the nameless narrator of Hugo's novel of early 1829, *The Last Day of a Condemned Man*, who cuts a universal figure in that his crime is never mentioned and who, echoing his author, reflects: "Condemned to death! Well, why not? *Men*, as I remember reading in some book or other in which that was the only good thing, *men are all condemned to death with indefinite stays of execution*. So what's so changed in my situation?"[17] But that condemned man well knew that, if his situation had not changed, he had: "Until the death sentence I had felt myself breathing, throbbing, living in the same milieu as other men; now I was clearly aware of a sort of confine between the world and myself. Nothing had the same look to me as before."[18] It remained for Stendhal's Julien under sentence of death not just to feel different, but to turn his former moral outlook topsy-turvy.

Subtextually, that death sentence on Julien is our universal mortality as in Pascal, and with Julien facing up to it as Pascal demanded. Pascal's death row is even graphic in Julien's case after the sentence is passed: "In bringing Julien back to prison they had put him into a cell reserved for those condemned to death."[19] On Julien's death row, however, Christian salvation is no option. The only grace is political, and Julien petitions for it solely on Madame de Rênal's account, reluctantly and without illusions. As if with a wink at Pascal, he refuses with pique to boost his appeal by converting. "In faith, if I meet the god of the Christians I'm lost, he is full of thoughts of reprisal," Julien reflects.[20] The misfire murderer accepts his fate as his just due for his intent to kill the woman whom he thereby discovered that he loves above all else. His earlier unawareness of this love is of a piece with his earlier inability to think of his days as numbered, however high or low their number. Christianity dies hard: the radical rift between Julien's worldliness before his crime and his unworldliness afterwards corresponds to the great Christian divide between this world and the next.

This radical rift reappears between the two women who mourn Julien. While Madame de Rênal follows him into death, succumbing to her grief, Mathilde entombs his severed head with macabre pomp and circumstance. Before falling for Julien way down below her haughty heights, Mathilde had once quipped to herself in her cult of a beheaded ancestor: "A death sentence is the one thing I can see that confers distinction on a man; it's the one thing that can't be bought."[21] The contrast between Mathilde loving Julien for his differentness and Madame de Rênal simply loving him parallels that between Julien's destiny singularized on the surface of the novel and, below its surface, normalized so as to stand for human mortality at large, or again between Stendhal historicizing on the one level of his novel and eternalizing on the other.

In high romantic style Alfred de Vigny reflected in his diary of 1832 that to bank on any joy was foolish in "this prison called life," which he posited in Pascal's own terms except that the execution at the end of it was for reasons unknown.[22] But the supreme romantic version of Pascal's paradigm of the death sentence defining the human condition was the Conciergerie scene in Georg Büchner's *Danton's Death* of 1835, with its pack of victims of France's Reign of Terror in early 1794 bracing to meet their fate; their protracted moment of truth is, however, one of heightened insight into the senselessness of all striving and suffering rather than, as with Julien, an existential flip throwing all their previous moral pointers into reverse. The Pascal paradigm, or death-row topos, lapsed with romanticism itself—gallows birds in fiction lost their universality[23]—then revived with the rash of ideologized butchery in Europe that began in 1914. It revived around the problem of guilt,[24] which the romantics had skirted or ignored even while they followed Pascal in construing natural death as an execution. With Christianity rejected, the Pauline problem of justifying death arose anew, though not until nearly a century after Stendhal and Büchner signed off, and then together with the Pauline solution of justifying death through inborn human sin, henceforth secularized as guilt.

The starter in this post-Christian revival was *The Trial* by Franz Kafka, which germinated punctually with the outbreak of World War I in 1914. Kafka's hero, unlike Julien Sorel, does not see the mysterious deadly proceedings instituted against him as founded, let alone revise his life's values in consequence. Such nonrevising of prior values was in fact the rule for this whole rich new crop of subtextual death rows in fiction. In Vladimir Nabokov's *Invitation to a Beheading* of 1934, the convict awaiting decapitation for "the most terrible of crimes, gnostical turpitude,"[25] repeatedly refuses to repent; indeed, he goes on refusing all the way to the executioner's block, from which he then surreally walks away. Equally consistent is the apathetic murderer in *The Stranger* of 1940 by Albert Camus before and after what he sees as only his "misfortune"[26] that will end on the scaffold. And in the 1948 drama *Montserrat* by Emmanuel Roblès, a Spanish commander in Venezuela in 1818, Izquierdo, has a set of random passers-by seized to be shot one by one unless and until his officer Montserrat, found to be in league with insurgent Bolivar, betrays the rebel's hideout. Izquierdo explains to the hostages: "You are guilty of . . . innocence,"[27] and tells unrelenting Montserrat that, heroics or no, he will be alone deep down in dying, "like all those who are agonizing at this hour the world over."[28] These are Roblès's two themes throughout, with no moral aboutface perceptible in any one of those rapid-fire innocent victims of fearful Izquierdo.

Yet some masterworks in this grim line do follow to a degree the existential precedent set by Stendhal's Julien. The Old Bolshevik being purged in Arthur Koestler's *Darkness at Noon* of 1940 does not, in his cell, disavow his life's service to the cause, but does finally look beyond its time-bound principles.[29] The chained murderer awaiting trial and sentencing in Jean Genet's *Deathwatch* of 1944 has been convulsed by his enchanted capital crime, as he shows his cellmates by a gyrating dance. Friedrich Dürrenmatt's shopkeeper in *The Visit* of 1955 and his commercial traveler in *The Breakdown* of 1956 are both delivered from banality through death sentences out of the blue. But closest of all to Stendhal's formula is "The Wall" of 1939 by Jean-Paul Sartre, with its three prisoners of the Spanish rebel armies under Franco awaiting the firing squad overnight. One has been condemned only for being a Loyalist's brother:

martial law is no pickier than death itself. Another, the narrator, relates: "Once I was going to die, nothing seemed natural to me any longer"[30]—a near echo of Hugo's condemned man as quoted earlier: "Nothing had the same look to me as before." In that tense interlude between life and death, Sartre's narrator feels estranged from his whole previous life. "I wondered how I had been able to stroll, to fool around with girls," he recollects; "I wouldn't have lifted a little finger had I imagined I'd die like that."[31] That estrangement projects into the hypothetical future: "In the state I was in, had they told me that I could just go home, that they let me off with my life, it would have left me cold: a few hours or a few years of waiting, it's all the same once you've lost the illusion of being eternal."[32] Yet it does not leave him cold when, by a fluke of fate, they do let him off with his life: his narrative ends abruptly with his burst of laughter at the news.

Stendhal's account of Julien in his death cell lacks the compelling immediacy of Sartre's narration of that long night of anguish beside the wall. But what Stendhal's depiction lacks in earthiness, it gains in symbolic power. Sartre's immediacy is just that, a spiritual pulse taking inside one of three trembling, sweating, smelling bodies; it fails to reach beyond the firing wall and bring the narrator's drastic revaluation of his past or possible future into focus. Facing execution, he would not have strolled, fooled around with girls, lifted a little finger. But no one not backed against the wall can live that way. On our figurative death row we live by ignoring where we are. When seen from Julien's death cell, the passions that had led up to his crime convey this evasiveness built into the normal course of life—an evasiveness amounting to falsity for which, since God's death, no remedy has availed. Camus made this same point *a contrario* in the first half of *The Stranger* through the narrator's primitive, paratactic account of the prehistory of his crime that turns it into a staccato succession of discrete perceptions, feelings, and acts each isolated in its instantaneity and hence unrelated to a prospective end of the series: removing the false connectives from life is itself an evasion. Camus himself later duly repudiated this stylistic artifice together with its absurd contrived effect as "a dead end."[33] It is in watching a credible hero closely as he lives first with and then without what Sartre's narrator in "The Wall" calls "the illusion of being eternal" that Stendhal's novel still stands alone.

By giving Pascal's parable of death row a post-Christian twist, Stendhal turned it into one of the two great modern tests for the sincerity of a life's course. On a par with it is Nietzsche's challenge: Would you live this moment differently if you were doomed to relive it in all eternity? To lend this question cosmic urgency, Nietzsche argued that, matter being finite and time infinite, every phenomenal configuration was bound to recur ad infinitum. His premises have since obsolesced without blunting his point. Where Nietzsche made his existential point outright, Stendhal made his fictionally through text and subtext together. In *The Red and the Black* (and again in *The Charterhouse of Parma*) Stendhal asked in effect: Would a death sentence change your life's priorities? Following Pascal, he added in effect: But you are now already condemned to death. For Stendhal, however, the afterworld was out, as passé as piquet, with no eternal recurrence or other ersatz afterlife replacing it: life was once only. Just this is what made his *Guillotinenromantik* (Büchner's apt word) modern and his chronicle of 1830 timeless.

NOTES

1. Stendhal, *Le rouge et le noir*, in *Romans et nouvelles*, vol. 1 (Paris: Pléiade, 1952), 526.

2. Ibid., 266. (This is how derivative Eugène de Rastignac in turn sizes up Madame de Nucingen in Balzac's *Old Goriot*.)

3. Ibid., 302.

4. Ibid., 503.

5. Ibid., 545.

6. Ibid., 651.

7. Ibid., 662.

8. Ibid., 690 (Stendhal's suspension points).

9. Ibid., 667.

10. Ibid., 695.

11. Ibid., 692.

12. Ibid. (Stendhal's suspension points).

13. Ibid., 649.

14. Christopher Marlowe, *Doctor Faustus*, IV.v.25.

15. Blaise Pascal, *Pensées*, in *Oeuvres complètes* (Paris: Pléiade, 1954), 1180, nos. 341, 342.

16. Victor Hugo, *Han d'Islande*, in *Oeuvres complètes* (Paris: Ollendorff, 1910), 320.

17. Victor Hugo, *Le dernier jour d'un condamné* (Paris: Hetzel, 1832), 49.

18. Ibid., 47. Stendhal read the novel as soon as it appeared and found it "horrifying": Stendhal, *Correspondance*, vol. 2, *1821–1834* (Paris: Pléiade, 1967), 161 (letter of 10 February 1829).

19. Stendhal, *Le rouge et le noir*, 676.

20. Ibid., 677. Further, 691: "that cruel little despot thirsting for vengeance."

21. Ibid., 489.

22. Alfred de Vigny, *Le journal d'un poète*, in *Oeuvres complètes*, vol. 2 (Paris: Pléiade, 1948), 945; also 946, 993.

23. A perfect illustration is Leonid Andreyev's *Story of Seven Who Were Hanged* (1908), the whole story being how each of these seven true culprits faces death differently.

24. On this revival in its post-Christian context, see my *After Christianity* (Durango, CO: Logbridge-Rhodes, 1986), 72–88.

25. Vladimir Nabokov, *Invitation to a Beheading*, trans. Dmitri Nabokov (New York: Putnam's, 1959), 72.

26. Albert Camus, *L'étranger*, in *Théâtre, récits, nouvelles* (Paris: Pléiade, 1962), 1166.

27. Emmanuel Roblès, *Montserrat* (Paris: Seuil, 1954), I:x.

28. Ibid., III:ix.

29. In *Spanish Testament* (London: Gollancz, 1937), Koestler recounted the inner upheaval wrought by his five days of solitary confinement under sentence of death from a military court in Malaga while five thousand other prisoners were shot, but this personal testimony did not take on a figurative meaning.

30. Jean-Paul Sartre, "Le mur," in *Le mur* (Paris: Gallimard, 1966), 23.

31. Ibid., 27.

32. Ibid., 28.

33. Quoted in Camus, *Théâtre, récits, nouvelles*, 1910, from an interview of 15 November 1945.

10

Like an Echo Fading
Flaubert's "A Simple Heart"

In "A Simple Heart" of 1875 Gustave Flaubert brought to perfection the literary realism that he had pioneered in *Madame Bovary* nearly twenty years before. Like that epochal novel, originally serialized in 1856, this newer gem of a tale recounts with studied dispassion a woman's life of tedium in the French provinces in the first part of the nineteenth century. But where Flaubert's earlier heroine, Emma Bovary, ends up a suicide by asking more of life than it can provide or than she can afford, his later, simple-hearted Félicité gives of herself unstintingly until from her death bed she contributes the tatters of her last precious worldly belonging to a Corpus Christi procession.

That pathetic donation is the remnants of Félicité's fourth and last love: her parrot Loulou, stuffed and mounted. Her first love is a peasant lad who tries to rape her, then proposes to her, only to marry a rich old lady instead. Jilted, the unschooled orphan and farmhand runs off in mortification to the nearest town. There she finds her life's work in keeping house for a stuffy widow and, at first, the widow's growing boy and girl. This girl, Virginie, is her second love. She secretly shares in Virginie's young life to the point of acquiring a naïve, impassioned piety from the girl's catechism lessons. Her third love is a nephew encountered by chance in his boyhood. She pampers him unsparingly out of her sparse means until he has become a sailor and departs on a distant voyage. He dies of yellow fever in Havana just as Virginie, nearly grown up by then, is succumbing to a wasting disease. Later exotic Loulou the parrot, left behind by a departing subprefect, is Félicité's perpetual companion; the attachment continues even after Loulou's death and, at a taxidermist's hands, resurrection. On her way to port by foot to dispatch dead Loulou to the taxidermist's, Félicité, who has been growing deaf, is thrown off the road by a mail coach that she does not hear coming. As she sits in pain pulling herself together, "her miserable childhood, her disappointed first love, her nephew's departure, Virginie's death,"[1] all well up within her—so many markers of an emotionally deprived existence. She survives her mistress by some years—stone deaf by then, eventually blind too, and alone. It is during that Corpus Christi procession to which she donates stuffed Loulou that she breathes her last while the beatific vision of a gigantic parrot hovers over her.

"A Simple Heart" lacks strict historic or regional definition: it would need little retouching to be reset in some other corner of France a generation earlier or later. Flaubert did, though, date the action circumstantially at a couple of junctures and did situate it specifically within his native Normandy. His simple-hearted heroine resembles any number of women of peasant stock in domestic service throughout Europe all that century. This he intended, yet he told her story with its whole run of small joys and great sorrows as if it were anchored in a unique time and place, bound to a given composite of objects, institutions, and usages acting on and through her, part and parcel of a single, definite social conformation itself intimately related to its physical environment, with her consciousness strictly reactive and her power of decision therefore illusory. His lesser characters, while never stereotypical, are likewise defined outwardly by their location in that particular ensemble of persons and places cohering organically, their salient moral traits being conceived as mere outgrowths of their total setting. Unwitting automatons, they appear the more so the more cursorily they are sketched. For all that, the characterizations carry no hint of condescension: in "A Simple Heart" as against his *Madame Bovary* or, above all, his comical *Bouvard and Pécuchet*, Flaubert's occasional faintly caricatural touches are almost affectionate. Least of all does it reflect on Félicité that she—this is how Flaubert introduces her—"looked like a wooden doll functioning mechanically,"[2] or that she should fit into an obscure niche or slot of existence just her size that is cheerless in its everyday sameness, sadness, and senselessness. On the contrary, her fate is moving just because she is helpless to shape or even to fathom it for herself.

Virtually any passage of "A Simple Heart" can illustrate Flaubert's peculiar intermix of a defining, if only loosely defined, human and material landscape. Take this chunk of his close-knit depiction of a family stay at Trouville early in Félicité's domestic service: "The principal diversion was the fishing boats returning. They always started to tack once they passed the buoys. With their sails two-thirds lowered and their foresails blown out like balloons, they would glide forward through the splashing waves to the middle of the harbor and abruptly drop anchor. Then they would each draw up to the pier, and the crew would throw its quivering catch ashore. There a line of carts would stand waiting, and women in cotton bonnets would rush to take the baskets and kiss the men."[3] This passage of Flaubert's narrative is typical even in being accessible without loss in isolation from the rest, like any stretch of a humdrum continuum. Flaubert's procedure, conspicuous here, of representing human conduct solely in its physical aspect assimilated to its physical setting pervades his entire tale. By its means he can turn even deeply personal experiences into natural occurrences, as he does in his vignette of those fishing boats returning. Witness Félicité's later aftershock from the impact of the mail coach that hurls her off the road with her dead parrot: painful pieces of her past, "like the waves of a rising tide, came back to her all at once and, welling up in her throat, choked her."[4] This deft seashore imagery follows the enumeration already quoted of her worst past sufferings, or rather of their outer causes ("her miserable childhood, her disappointed first love, her nephew's departure, Virginie's death"[5]). These hurts are thereby so reified that it would have traduced Flaubert's intention had I called them "her painful memories," as if they were purely mental instead of palpably afflicting her as they rise out of her inner depths. In this objectifying idiom, the physical can just as readily double for the mental, as when Félicité lies dying: "Her heartbeats grew slower, each one fainter and gentler, like a fountain running dry, like an echo fading."[6]

By applying such a narrative mode to a simple-hearted social victim and cultural nobody, Flaubert aimed to convey the tragic mindlessness of all human life trapped within its confining and constraining circumstances. "Tragic" may sound overstated for that regular, everyday onlooking by vacationers (their "principal diversion") which introduces Flaubert's elegant depiction of fishing boats returning to port complete with the clockwork kissing that tops it off. But that elegance is all Flaubert's, distilled from the daily routines of vacationers and fishermen's wives acting in concert with the fishing boats and, subordinate to the boats themselves, their crews. As far as Flaubert's account discloses—and this is the studied stylistic point of it—the crews might not be sailing the boats but the boats instead sailing the crews, or the sea sailing both, with the female accessories correspondingly conditioned, or programmed, to deliver their kisses on schedule, never mind how those kisses feel. Moreover, this daily fishing spectacle appears in Flaubert's text not for its own picturesque sake, but as a stock item of local scenery available to Félicité and her party day in, day out, between the rising and the setting sun, with the sun's own unthinking regularity. This fishing sequence conjoining persons with their appurtenances, and with animals and the elements, in a typically uneventful passage of Félicité's derivative life, contains in miniature the overall conception of the tale. In Flaubert's scheme of things, a life defined that way, like a piece of natural history, is tragic.

But what is the interest of such a simple life that is tragic in its issueless inner poverty? The pathetic futility of a fate defined by its singularized social and material context, and hence distinctly not our own, is no very promising theme for a readership of all times and climes. And Flaubert's perfected account of that empty life unfolding, his placid, steady, leveling gaze at the specific constituents of its emptiness, his recording them blandly and succinctly one by one so that their pathetic futility keeps showing: all this could engage only the belletrist for long. The appeal of "A Simple Heart" lies rather in Flaubert's winning combination of text with subtext. In his text, as already stated, Félicité's miserable life is a running effect, a dependent function, of its context that is pointedly not ours. Our sympathy accordingly traverses a critical existential distance from Félicité staked out by Flaubert: we feel how unlike us she is in all that makes her fate so affecting. The subtext, though, turns this distancing achieved through the text topsy-turvy. For subtextually that lowly life represents, on the contrary, the soft core of every human life, the inside story of all our existences, however diverse, complex, or sophisticated.

What life is lived without some disappointment in love? After Félicité is introduced as a peerless maidservant of over a half-century's standing, a flashback begins: "Like any woman, she had had her love story."[7] Here in a nutshell is Flaubert's two-tiered realism: while that coming love story is Félicité's alone, its baseline is everyone's. Flaubert's wording here is even pithier to this effect than English allows. "Like any woman" has the force of "like anyone else" in the original ("comme une autre"), being feminine only as French grammar requires and to no restrictive effect.[8] That first, luckless love of Félicité's is reciprocated, as are her three loves that follow, only incommensurably, return love being disproportionate in the nature of things. And what life escapes grief for the dead? Acute status consciousness on both sides, if nothing else, keeps Félicité at a proper remove from her mistress over her half-century's service except once, when a sudden shared remembrance of dead Virginie bridges that social gap to end in a kiss "that made them equal."[9] Here too the French "qui les égalisait," with its suggestion of leveling out or reducing to parity, makes its all-human point more sharply than English permits. Loulou is differentness itself, which is the soul of every pet we love. Yet Félicité's spiritual traffic with dead Loulou is the common lot of the bereaved, magnified—the materialist's secret, writ large. Similarly, Félicité's childlike, magical religiosity is just her one of the illusions that sustain all our lives. And her thankless workaday drudgery and off-hours sacrifices—her daily household toiling and skimping for her mistress, her tending Polish refugees and nursing a cancerous old derelict—epitomize the ultimate evanescence and futility of our finest labors in that fullness of cosmic time that preyed on Flaubert's mind and, behind all our pressing preoccupations, preys on ours.

But Flaubert's exposure of the tragic vanity of existence in "A Simple Heart" cuts still deeper. For, on his construction, the very stuff and substance of Félicité's existence, unique like any existence, is the specific trivia enumerated by him at a leisurely, even pace, with its few big moments integrated into that smooth and seamless narrative. Take this description of a pattern of outings early along in Félicité's domestic service:

> When the sky was clear, they would set off early for the farm at Geffosses.
> The farmyard there is on a slope, with the house in the middle; and the sea, in the distance, looks like a streak of grey.
> Félicité would take some slices of cold meat out of her basket, and they would eat their lunch in a room adjoining the dairy. It was the last remnant of a country house now forsaken. The wallpaper, in tatters, fluttered in the breeze. Madame Aubain would lean forward, bowed down with memories; the children did not dare to speak. "Play, why don't you?" she would say, and off they would go.[10]

This passage, with its present tense for a stable landscape in between its incantatory imperfects for what the excursionists would habitually do, actually leads up to a dramatic, memorable incident in which Félicité selflessly saves the family from a charging bull. Even at the height of this suspenseful event Flaubert's imperfects still manage to predominate, their slow, smooth, sonorous rhythms unbroken. That family holiday at the seashore follows, all in repetitive imperfects now, including its "principal diversion" of watching the day's fishing reach its daily end.

This subtle play of tenses, with the imperfects providing a basic tonality that absorbs the sprinkle of simple pasts and rare presents, exemplifies the mastery with which Flaubert could compose a tableau in slow motion, a recurrent doing, a whole way of life, out of physical externals painstakingly particularized, almost any one of which could nonetheless be changed without loss. The farm house at Geffosses could be pushed to one side of the slope, the sliced meat turned into cheese, the picnic room split off from the dairy; Madame Aubain could lean her head sidewise either way—except that then her memories would forego some of that palpable, ponderous gravity imputed to them. Paradoxically, by this practice of arbitrary denotation Flaubert created an atmosphere of the *un*importance of the just-what, just-when, just-where, or just-how that constitute any life history and that at the same time were his exclusive building blocks for Félicité's entire story.

Flaubert's subtext transpires, then, not so much through that life story itself as through the language that conveys it. In his realistic prose Flaubert sought, and in "A Simple Heart" he achieved, graphic, limpid, lucid transparency, a straight, unproblematic look at life, a picture in writing free of all authorial presence or impress, undercutting any and every point of view, with no word or phrase obtruding and no meanings or values added. This was ex-God's absolute perspective cast as prose—at least short of Flaubert's somber stress, reminiscent of Ecclesiastes, on the senseless recurrences built into creation.

In privileging recurrence as it did, Flaubert's stylistic reconstruction of life, or construction on life, was inimical to radical change. So too on its terms does the past, rather than lengthening or deepening over time, wipe itself out: thus "the years went by, all alike"[11] after Virginie's death. By syntactical sleight of hand Flaubert could even get Félicité to go blind uneventfully: "But, blind by then, she. . . ."[12] He triumphed in just such loaded phrases that mostly, like Félicité's days and years, pass unnoticed. The *mot juste* that he notoriously would agonize after was not the most, but more nearly the least, conspicuous word on any one of his pages. Paradoxically again, his style was itself a corrective for its own depressive import. For it redeemed the inanity of a world that it rendered with a fastidiously textured just-right-ness foreshadowing that height of unrealism: fin-de-siècle art for art's sake. That texture carried over intact beyond realism into the rich artistry of his "Saint Julian Hospitator" and especially "Herodias," the second and third of his *Three Tales* of which "A Simple Heart" was the first.

Life stripped of all subjective adornments or defensive illusions, as it is in Flaubert's prose, is unlivable. This implication of "A Simple Heart" emerges the more starkly where now and again even Flaubert's stylistic subtlety lapsed. Lapse it did into a near pastiche of itself in the report, gleaned from a sea captain, of Félicité's nephew's death: "At the hospital they had bled him too much for yellow fever. Four doctors at once held him. He died immediately, and the head doctor said, 'Well, there goes one more!' "[13] Equally unsubtle is this line that concludes a bare-bones account of Félicité tending her human wreck of a derelict: "He died, and she had a mass said for the repose of his soul."[14] To have written just "for him" instead of "for the repose of his soul" would have cut the thought too short. In the event, Flaubert overloaded the sentence with that all-too-ironic tack-on after he had reduced the derelict groveling in a ruined pig-sty to a mere inflamed, coughing, drooling, trembling residue of a huge burst tumor. Flaubert's effects were all contrived at the cost of Promethean toil, but just these couple of failed effects in "A Simple Heart" were wanting in the supreme artifice of looking uncontrived.

Life's inanity as a trick of style, as a message artfully encoded in one inconspicuous pick of words or turn of phrase after another: even this was not the whole subtextual story of "A Simple Heart." The tale conveys something additional just as poignantly at the metaphysical gut level and conveys it with an exquisite irony due to Flaubert's mastery of language: the vanity of speech, the nullity of dialogue, above all the incommunicability of our innermost experience. In other works Flaubert scored satiric points by having his characters talk out of his own lifelong collection of clichés, his *Dictionary of Received Ideas*; in "A Simple Heart" he cut talk down instead to its vacuous essentials. The first full sentence spoken in the tale is Félicité's when her failed rapist begins a false courtship, itself recounted in indirect discourse: " 'Ah!' she said."[15] Soon after that, just as a cart driver is pointing out the house into which that false suitor married, his chatter is drowned out by his horses' clatter. This running theme of speech depleted or deleted without loss comes to a head when Félicité goes deaf: "Every living being moved about in ghostly silence."[16] Here was the realist's world reduced to its basic elements: life with the sound track removed, with people cut down to their physiology, their action tending to pantomime as it flattens out into a dumb show, into mere gesture on the surface of life. In this same vein, Félicité's one-sided conversations with Loulou continue unabated for all her growing deafness, even as "the little circle of her ideas narrowed still further."[17] At last she hears only the piercing voice of her parrot reciting his scant repertory of parroted phrases, and she replies "in words no more coherent but straight from the heart."[18] These words, like Loulou's, are others' phrases reechoed, as is all common parlance: such is the pathetic sense of her heartbeat eventually dying "like an echo fading."[19] Her miserable equivalent of communication continues in silence, through the eyes, with dead Loulou perched atop her mantelpiece beside an image of the Holy Ghost. Her blindness, finally, closes off this last way out of herself short of her deathbed vision of Loulou as the Holy Ghost. For Flaubert as against his Félicité, that God who once saw to the heart of us was no more, and at that inexpressibility of our innermost being Flaubert designedly brought his power of words to a halt.

Just as Félicité made of her Loulou a symbol of all spiritual being, Flaubert made of his Félicité a figure of humanity as a whole stripped down to its simple heart. The universe contracts for Félicité around her parrot before opening out onto eternity through her parrot. And Flaubert, to depict Félicité's cosmic-scaled idolatry, set himself up for weeks on end facing a stuffed parrot. He had remarked of his first great heroine, whose sensibility he shared: "Emma Bovary, c'est moi." He might have maintained with more obvious justification:

"Félicité, c'est nous tous." For Félicité represents us all at bottom, in those vital depths where socialization, intellect, and sensibility cease to divide us.

Flaubert's realism prior to "A Simple Heart" can also be called natural symbolism. Its principle was that any specimen of a commonplace entity, rightly chosen and rendered, stood for its whole kind. That "rightly" slanted the operation just a little, but no matter: Emma Bovary was all the more typical of provincial housewifery for being at the extreme of quiet desperation. Flaubert's realism in "A Simple Heart" was something else again. Félicité is no "average type"—the statistical concept that appears to have influenced Flaubert's earlier realism. She is, rather, a least common denominator. Hers are the rudiments of all human attachment and detachment, fantasy and frustration, loving and losing. But—to repeat this crucial point—she is this universal figure subtextually only; textually she is uniquely herself, meaning nobody else, and thereby proof against Flaubert's readers' identifying with her.

On this single score of all-human universality, Flaubert's maturest realism rejoined the high classicism of Racine so radically unlike it otherwise, what with Racine's majestic aloofness from the commonplace, the humble, the workaday, and all the material specifics of person and surroundings that constituted Félicité's very identity. But Phaedra's universality was writ large in Racine's text. That in Racine's play Phaedra's virtue is no match for the vice within her meant outright, textually, that virtue is no match for vice, period. Racine's subtext took off from that surface universalism, as from a premise, to equate love with vice. In "A Simple Heart," by contrast, the universality is strictly subtextual. Félicité touches our depths because her simple heart is our heart at its simplest, though Félicité's beats in tune with a physique and a mentality, a status and an occupation, a locale and a period, that are as far from ours as Flaubert could make them right in our midst.

"As far from ours" was perforce as far downward from ours. For snobbery plays its part even in literary form. A Racine set his high and mighty tragic personages at a still-loftier remove than their Greek originals from all mean concerns, alone with their quintessential passions. With such grand figures we readily identify upward. On the other hand, we are unable to identify with Félicité at the level of text not just because she is concretized against all the Racinian rules, but still more because she is the polar opposite of high and mighty. Flaubert distanced her from any reader at all by making her illiterate and from any likely reader by the menial character and narrow confines of her humble existence. His text, for all its unsentimental sobriety, invites sympathy downward for that untutored mind and tender soul with its touching credulity, its unrequited giving, and its frustrated loving. At the same time, that distance downward is a barrier against our identifying with her outright. Only subtextually does our common humanity prevail.

NOTES

1. Gustave Flaubert, "Un coeur simple," in *Trois contes*, in *Oeuvres*, vol. 2 (Paris: Pléiade, 1952), 616. A fine English rendition of this work is Gustave Flaubert, *Three Tales*, trans. Robert Baldick (London: Penguin, 1961).

2. Flaubert, "Un coeur simple," 592.

3. Ibid., 600.

4. Ibid., 616.

5. Ibid.

6. Ibid., 622.

7. Ibid., 592.

8. To be sure, Flaubert could have written "comme tout le monde" ("like everybody") to make his point gender-free at some cost of neatness and euphony. So he just may have meant a "love story" in the singular to be the common lot of women more than of men even if his other works hardly support that distinction.

9. Flaubert, "Un coeur simple," 611.

10. Ibid., 596.

11. Ibid., 610.

12. Ibid., 620.

13. Ibid., 607 (arguably still more callous in Flaubert's original: "Bon! encore un!").

14. Ibid., 612.

15. Ibid., 593.

16. Ibid., 615.

17. Ibid.

18. Ibid.

19. Ibid., 622.

Mankind Revisited
Dostoyevsky's "The Grand Inquisitor"

Fyodor Dostoyevsky's most celebrated creation is an unwritten poem. Called "The Grand Inquisitor," it forms part of his last and greatest novel, *The Brothers Karamazov*. The passage containing it was the May 1879 installment when the novel emerged serially in a Russian journal that year and the next. That passage is often read and discussed separately from the rest of the novel, yet it is closely enough integrated into the surrounding narrative that it cannot be excerpted with a clear-cut beginning or end. Its larger novelistic context is vital, moreover, for clarifying its otherwise enigmatic message.

"The Grand Inquisitor" comes into the action of *The Brothers Karamazov* a day after the aging debauchee Fyodor Karamazov, delighted at his dinner by a disputation about Christianity between two of his domestics, frowns strangely afterwards, dismisses the disputants, and with sudden, unaccustomed, cognac-drenched gravity, asks his two sons present whether God and immortality exist. The one, rationalistic Ivan, answers no and no; the other, pious Alyosha, yes and yes. The following evening these two brothers, who have grown up separately, resume this very Russian discussion of ultimates between just the two of them by way of getting to know each other better. Ivan, reminded that he denied God the night before, maintains that he was just teasing: maybe he accepts God after all. Asked whether he is joking again, Ivan says no, he really does accept the same Christian god as Alyosha, only he rejects the world that this god made. By way of clarifying his position, Ivan adds that whereas he can love his neighbors only abstractly or impersonally, he cannot abide innocent human suffering, especially by children. No transcendent retribution, he insists, can ever make good the drastic existential pain and anguish of any one of the children molested to death day in, day out in the common run of life. Poignantly he declares against a higher cosmic harmony at that price: "For love of mankind I don't want it."[1] As Alyosha duly brings up redemption through Christ, Ivan counters with that poem he once imagined but never penned, "The Grand Inquisitor," relating it in potent, solemn prose interrupted by only a few exchanges with Alyosha, all of them insignificant except the last one.

Ivan's poem is set in Seville at the height of the Inquisition. There, on the morrow of a splendid auto-da-fé, Jesus appears in the cathedral square, radiating love and compassion. The townsfolk flock around him in reverent joy. In his presence a blind man's sight is restored, and he calls a girl in an open coffin back to life. Soon the aged Grand Inquisitor approaches, scowling, and orders the miracle worker seized and imprisoned. The crowd makes way submissively as a captive Jesus is led away. That night the Inquisitor visits Jesus in his cell and tells him that the same crowd that had kissed his feet will stoke the coals on the morrow when he is burned at the stake for hindering the church's work. This work, the Inquisitor declares, consists in supplanting Christ's teaching of free moral choice as recorded in the Gospels with strict priestly control over the conduct and consciences of the masses for their own good. For, he explains, most people are base, weak, credulous, and unruly, incapable of earthly happiness if left to run wild, let alone of salvation on Christ's demanding terms of personal responsibility. At bottom, humans are herd animals harboring a perverse impulse to break loose from the herd. If ever they are to live in peace and contentment, they need bread, authority, and a common faith dogmatically dispensed from a single source. Christ, however, by refusing Satan's threefold temptation to turn stones into bread, ensnare souls by miracles, and rule by the sword, abandoned the weak and depraved multitude to its misery for the sake of the blessed few who could follow him by due personal choice. But those superior few, from pity for the teeming, suffering rabble abandoned by heaven, have gradually taken it upon themselves to serve Satan's humane purpose as against Christ's elitist conceit. This commiserate clerisy is accordingly twisting its sacerdotal office in Christ's own name to the end of organizing Christendom into a harmonious anthill of boundless creatural bliss against Christ's intent. One day the ecclesiastical power brokers will run the lives of the weak and wicked for them definitively—so the

Inquisitor next assures his prisoner—permitting them even to sin in all innocence,

and as for the punishment for these sins, very well, we take it upon ourselves . . . and we will decide all things, and they will joyfully believe our decision, because it will deliver them from their great care and their present terrible torments of personal and free decision. And everyone will be happy, all the millions of creatures, except for the hundred thousand of those who govern them. For only we, we who keep the mystery, only we shall be unhappy. There will be thousands of millions of happy babes, and a hundred thousand sufferers who have taken upon themselves the curse of the knowledge of good and evil. Peacefully they will die, peacefully they will expire in your name, and beyond the grave they will find only death. But we will keep the secret, and for their own happiness we will entice them with a heavenly and eternal reward. For even if there were anything in the next world, it would not, of course, be for such as they. It is said and prophesied that you will come and once more be victorious, you will come with your chosen ones, with your proud and mighty ones, but we will say that they saved only themselves, while we have saved everyone. It is said that the harlot who sits upon the beast and holds *mystery* in her hands will be disgraced, that the feeble will rebel again, that they will tear her purple and strip bare her "loathsome" body. But then I will stand up and point out to you the thousands of millions of happy babes who do not know sin. And we, who took their sins upon ourselves for their happiness, we will stand before you and say: "Judge us if you can and dare." Know that I am not afraid of you. Know that I too was in the wilderness, and I too ate locusts and roots; that I too blessed freedom, with which you have blessed mankind, and I too was preparing to enter the number of your chosen ones, the number of the strong and mighty, with a thirst "that the number be complete." But I awoke and did not want to serve madness. I returned and joined the host of those who have *corrected your deed*.[2]

The Inquisitor concludes his monologue by reiterating his death sentence against the captive Christ, and Ivan pauses. Alyosha thereupon pours out objections to the Inquisitor's complaints against Christ, concluding: "Your Inquisitor doesn't believe in God, that's his whole secret!"[3] Ivan nominally agrees: "At last you've understood. Yes, indeed, that alone is the whole secret."[4] In reply, Alyosha tells Ivan impulsively in great sorrow, as if Ivan and his Inquisitor were one: "You don't believe in God."[5] In his next breath Alyosha asks how the poem ends, and Ivan answers:

I was going to end it like this: when the Inquisitor fell silent, he waited some time for his prisoner to reply. His silence weighed on him. He had seen how the captive listened to him all the while intently and calmly, looking him straight in the eye, and apparently not wishing to contradict anything. The old man would have liked him to say something, even something bitter, terrible. But suddenly he approaches the old man in silence and gently kisses him on his bloodless, ninety-year-old lips. That is the whole answer. The old man shudders. Something stirs at the corner of his mouth; he walks to the door, opens it, and says to him: "Go and do not come again . . . do not come at all . . . never, never!" And he lets him out into the "dark squares of the city." The prisoner goes away.[6]

As for the Inquisitor, Ivan later adds: "The kiss burns in his heart, but the old man holds to his former idea."[7] This kiss burning in the Inquisitor's heart as Ivan's poem ends brings it full circle back to the love burning in Christ's heart as the poem begins.[8]

"The Grand Inquisitor" casts some scorching light on our vile, childish, wayward human breed that, even so, the Inquisitor loves and serves after his fashion. Perhaps it casts its light at the wrong angle, as no imaginable amount or kind of governance such as the Inquisitor advocates to correct Christ's deed could prevent there ever again being "just one . . . tortured child,"[9] and just one child ever tortured would suffice on Ivan's own terms to vitiate any such correction of Christ's deed as the Inquisitor proposes. But Ivan's poetry exceeds his politics. What makes this work-within-a-work so fascinating and puzzling both at once is not its rationale for inquisitorial rule, nor even the light it casts on the human breed at the right or wrong angle; to mimic the Inquisitor (himself quoting Revelation), that is not where the "*mystery*" of it lies. That mystery turns rather on a question that runs right through it subjacently, which is the very question that tormented Dostoyevsky all his life: whether God exists, or specifically whether the Christian God exists along with the Christian afterlife.

On the face of it, the Christian God does indeed exist in "The Grand Inquisitor," for in it Christ revisits the world. That is its fixed point of departure. In a literary preface spoken to Alyosha, Ivan expressly places his poem in a rich medieval tradition ("I don't need to mention Dante"[10]) that takes a human visit to or from God as its first term of reference. By his very presence in sixteenth-century Seville, Christ—identified by the narrative voice in the poem straight off, recognized on all sides, replaying a couple of his miracles more or less faithfully—stands warrant for his own supernatural reality and hence for the objective truth of the whole Christian package. The Inquisitor in particular, after an initial, equivocal saving clause ("whether it is you, or only his likeness"[11]), consistently acknowledges Christ to his face. To puzzled Alyosha, Ivan nonetheless concedes that the Inquisitor may be fantasizing Christ's appearance in Seville and then asks: "But isn't it all the same?"[12] No, it is not. In humoring Alyosha this way, Ivan concedes too much. For the Inquisitor to be only imagining Christ would contradict the unequivocal narrative—and besides, then the people of Seville, who "recognize him,"[13] would have to be imagining him as well. In any case, the fable is invariably read as Ivan's fantasy and never as the Inquisitor's.

So this fable of Ivan's has it that Christ is palpably there gently facing off the irate Inquisitor in Seville. Further, most of what the Inquisitor tells Christ there in Seville complements what Ivan has told Alyosha just before relating the poetic fable. Ivan had objected to God's world on the ground of the innocent human suffering it contains; the Inquisitor adds that Christ, with due love, could have done as Satan proposed and delivered the wretched multitude from its earthly misery had he not loftily preferred to save just an unhappy saintly few on his elitist terms. So God botched his original creation, and Christ his salvaging mission, for want of sufficient love of humankind: thus Ivan. To quote Dostoyevsky's overemphatic notes for the Inquisitor's defiant confrontation with Christ: "I LOVE HUMANITY MORE THAN YOU DO."[14] But halt: in the Christian perspective God is love; the love that is God extends to all God's creatures equally; in Ivan's Seville that love fittingly burns in Christ's heart and radiates from his visage; inside his prison cell it even issues in a kiss on his raging enemy's lips. So the loving God *could* not generate, and his loving son *could* not perpetuate, innocent human suffering for the sake of what Ivan calls "eternal harmony" or again "someone's future harmony," meaning just to suit that same God's metaphysical purposes.[15] Therefore the Christian God and, by the same token, his filial incarnation and retributory afterworld do not exist. This forced implication, mostly undrawn, is Ivan's subtext to "The Grand Inquisitor," which by Ivan's authorial design and for "a Euclidean mind, an earthly mind" like his own[16] shows right through his gripping image of divine love incarnate afoot in Seville.

Let me take that again, schematizing Ivan's tricky position. Ours is a world unworthy of claiming the Christian God of love as its creator. Consequently that omnipotent, omniscient God either flubbed the creation and the redemption for all his omniscience and omnipotence or else, more logically, he does not exist. The first is the overt, the second the covert, argument of Ivan's imaginary poem—its text and subtext respectively.

For consistency's sake, then, the atheism in Ivan's poem should be, and mostly is, strictly subtextual. Ivan equivocates accordingly when troubled Alyosha exclaims: "Your Inquisitor doesn't believe in God, that's his whole secret!" Ivan promptly agrees, but only to echo Alyosha's words with a tiny, crucial change, saying: "That alone is the whole secret"[17]—the secret of the poem, that is, and not the Inquisitor's secret, which would be pointless paradox. Never once does Ivan's Inquisitor doubt the stark and urgent reality of God and Satan, salvation and damnation. Least of all does he doubt their reality when, in joining the devil's party for love of sinful mankind, he—as Ivan next tells Alyosha—saw the need to "accept lies and deceit, and lead people, consciously now, to death and destruction, deceiving them, moreover, all along the way, so that they somehow do not notice where they are being led, so that at least on the way these pitiful, blind men consider themselves happy. And deceive them, notice, in the name of him in whose ideal the old man believed so passionately all his life."[18] With this conversion to the devil's humane cause the Inquisitor repudiates Christ and salvation without even beginning to deny their reality. Quite the contrary, he chooses universal felicity for humankind in the here-and-now at the posted price of certain "death and destruction" for the "pitiful and blind" masses misled into sin and, in the bargain, at the same price for his own apostatic party as well. Indeed, he has his defiant apologia ready in so many words to hurl at the whole heavenly host on Judgment Day. In sum, Ivan's Inquisitor acknowledges an all-too-actual God in giving him a calling down to his face the tacit logic or illogic of which is that he doesn't exist.

The Inquisitor's case for constructing that harmonious anthill to (half quoting now) correct Christ's deed does not take that penalty of automatic "death and destruction" for its beneficiaries into full and proper account. Or does the Inquisitor mean that only those who, like him, renounce salvation to give their weaker fellows an earthly boost would have been capable of salvation anyhow? He could not know this, but his reasoning collapses otherwise. For if some of those numberless happy babes might have qualified for salvation had he not herded them into his satanic anthill, then whatever that anthill's brutish benefits, he would thereby have done them only a dubious short-term favor.

For a fleeting moment the Inquisitor seems to take the tack that not just salvation, but immortality itself, is reserved for the chosen few exclusively—that "beyond the grave" the poor sinners, and they alone, "will find only death." But that fleeting moment ends abruptly at the anomalous words "even if there were anything in the next world," which imply with no two ways about it that there is an all-around nothing beyond the grave after all for both saint and sinner. In Dostoyevsky's notes for this passage the Inquisitor goes still further and tells Christ "that those who suffer his cross will not find anything that had been promised exactly as he himself had not found anything after his cross."[19] Is this nothingness hereafter the secret of the Inquisitor's this-worldly commitment, a secret that the final text lets slip out of him only at the peak of his rhetoric? This would mean that he did not believe anyway in the salvation that, after eating locusts and roots in the wilderness, he came to refuse for suffering humanity's sake. Such an ad hoc construction on his passing denial of a next world would render the poem as a whole meaningless. Besides, had the outspoken Inquisitor suspected Christ of only fooling mankind with tidings of life eternal, he would have said so; as it is, he proudly claims this deception as the church's. Nor does Ivan suspect Christ of lying about the afterlife. Ivan questions only Christ's existence and values, never his veracity. For him, Christianity is all one: if Christ, then also Satan and sin along with that crack at salvation for our miserable earthly breed. Later in the novel Ivan hallucinates a visit from the devil, who, his existence thus falsely manifest, wonders accordingly "whether proof of the devil is also proof of God"[20]—a witty reflection on "The Grand Inquisitor" with its visit from Christ fantasized by Ivan complete with an implicit denial of the visitor's existence. But at this earlier stage of the novel the universal death eternal that creeps into the Inquisitor's speech, and that Ivan then confirms to Alyosha on the Inquisitor's behalf, is simply and patently out of place—in brief, a mistake.

Whose mistake is this death eternal that doesn't fit? Not the Inquisitor's, for Ivan confirms it afterwards to Alyosha on the Inquisitor's account. Nor, since Ivan does confirm it, can the narrative voice in the poem be usefully distinguished on this score from Ivan's own. So the slipup is Ivan's, prompted by his deep doubts about God's existence that register in the subtext of his poem. His denial of God is in fact the downside of his seesawing about God throughout this sequence of the brotherly reunion. Having voiced that denial flatly at dinner the night before, he retracts it only ambiguously to Alyosha before reciting "The Grand Inquisitor," for to that retraction he shortly adds: "I long ago decided not to think about whether man created God or God created man."[21] His denial next creeps into the text of his poem vicariously through that slipup about the empty afterworld, then equivocally into his discussion of the poem with Alyosha when, in agreeing about the Inquisitor that atheism is "his whole secret," he drops the "his." That atheism, the secret of his poem, is also the inner logic of the stand Ivan takes with Alyosha before he brings up the poem—of his rejection of the moral scheme of the world as unworthy of God. Well beyond this single episode of "The Grand Inquisitor," moreover, Ivan's conflicted atheism is a running overt theme of the entire novel. Hence the Inquisitor's sudden, implicit, incongruous denial of life beyond death, with Ivan half confirming it afterwards, strongly argues that this blunder by torn Ivan was deliberate on Dostoyevsky's part, Ivan's ambivalence having quite consciously been Dostoyevsky's own. It argues the same way that whereas in Dostoyevsky's writing notes Ivan's uncertain atheism came into "The Grand Inquisitor" less deviously and more aggressively, in the end Dostoyevsky relegated it at this juncture of the novel almost entirely to Ivan's psychic underground and to the subtext of Ivan's poem. Artistically, Dostoyevsky's subtler lapse-of-logic technique, his deftly crafted blunder by the Inquisitor seconded by Ivan, is more than justified, for "The Grand Inquisitor," by being presented as ambivalent Ivan's unborn brainchild, strikes readers as altogether coherent, however baffling or unfathomable.

It is the conjunction of an atheistic subtext with the overt textual presence of Christ in all his exceeding humanity and divinity combined that lends Ivan's poem its uncanny, even nightmarish, intensity. The Inquisitor letting slip to Christ in Seville that heaven is a fable is of a venerable kind with Christopher Marlowe's Doctor Faustus in Wittenberg telling the devil he conjures up from below: "I think hell's a fable."[22] But beyond even a Marlowe's audacity, and dizzyingly deeper, is the conflation in Ivan's poem of a silent Christ with an unspoken disproof of his existence. For Ivan inwardly, against his own rationalistic rules of evidence, seeing need not be believing. His Christ does appear, but under the sign of fiction only. Later in the novel Ivan demands of his hallucinated devil with fierce insistence: "Is there a God, or not?" When the devil begs off, saying: "I just don't know," Ivan cries: "You don't know, yet you see God? . . . You are *me, me* and nothing else! . . . You are my fantasy!"[23] Just so Christ in Seville was Ivan's fantasy, and Ivan was Dostoyevsky's fantasy—these latter two fantasies conceived, though, unlike Ivan's devil, at a fever pitch short of delirium.

"Conflation" may be too static, too placid, a term for Ivan's Christ at once sublimely present and yet refuted. The text of "The Grand Inquisitor" denouncing God's bungled creation and Christ's bungled mission intermixes only uneasily, only in dynamic tension, with its subtext asserting the falsity of Christianity. In the text, moreover, the calling down of Christ is offset by the figure of unearthly holiness that he cuts, while the subtextual refutation of God, though strictly deductive, has the look of a grievance against him. These crossed tendencies reflect the ambivalence, or conflicting impulses, behind them. This ambivalence was first off Dostoyevsky's own vacillation between piety and skepticism, each pushing the other to a drastic extreme. So personal is ambivalence even where, as here, it touches an all-human nerve, and even where, as here, one of its two terms is disavowed, that its expression, however fine artistically, never fails to conjure up a particular human being behind it. But Dostoyevsky, unlike Goethe in *Werther* or Goethe's romantic epigones, shied away from novelistic self-display. In *The Brothers Karamazov* Dostoyevsky depersonalized his ambivalence about Christianity first by assigning its two terms to Alyosha and to Ivan respectively. But then his masterstroke in that masterwork was to project his ambivalence onto Ivan separately as well, and through Ivan into Ivan's poem in the form of a text at loggerheads with its subtext—a poem in which God's explicit existence is undercut by his implicit nonexistence.

With this winning combination, Dostoyevsky was at last satisfied with a piece of his own writing. And with all its ambivalence, that piece of his writing has thrilled the world ever since.

NOTES

1. Fyodor Dostoyevsky, *The Brothers Karamazov*, trans. by Richard Pevear and Larissa Volokhonsky (New York: Alfred A. Knopf, 1992), 245.

2. Ibid., 259–60.

3. Ibid., 261.

4. Ibid.

5. Ibid., 262.

6. Ibid.

7. Ibid.

8. Ibid., 249: "shines." But Dostoyevsky's text reads "burns" ("gorit") in both cases.

9. Dostoyevsky, 245–46.

10. Ibid., 246.

11. Ibid., 250.

12. Ibid.

13. Ibid.

14. Edward Wasiolek, trans. and ed., *The Notebooks for the Brothers Karamazov* (Chicago: University of Chicago Press, 1971), 75.

15. Dostoyevsky, 235, 236; 244.

16. Ibid., 235.

17. Ibid., 261. Russian having no "the," Dostoyevsky simply but conspicuously omitted "his."

18. Ibid., 261.

19. Wasiolek, 82.

20. Dostoyevsky, 637.

21. Ibid., 235.

22. Christopher Marlowe, *Doctor Faustus*, II.i.133.

23. Dostoyevsky, 642.

12

A Lamed and Tamed Duck
Ibsen's *The Wild Duck*

"Marriage . . . has ruined the human race."
From Ibsen's first note for *The Wild Duck*[1]

The Wild Duck, a drama of 1884 by Henrik Ibsen, makes two big points at once, one loudly and one quietly. It makes them both through naturalistic action and dialogue. But for good measure it also compacts them symbolically into a wild duck that has a side story figurative of the main story. That web-footed title character holds the stage for most of the play and even cuts in on the climax without ever quite appearing.

The wild duck belongs to the Ekdals, a family consisting of an aged, tippling, broken former officer, then forester, then convict; his windy son, Hjalmar; Hjalmar's wife, Gina, who runs their poor household and photographic studio; and adolescent Hedvig, Gina's daughter by a big businessman named Håkon Werle. The Ekdals' family background shows right through a piteous foreground from the outset. Gina had kept house for Werle while his demented wife lay dying and while he stood trial for felling state timber in partnership with Ekdal. The two partners faced charges together, but guileless Ekdal alone was jailed—and never quite knew what hit him. Then Werle, having won acquittal at Ekdal's expense, launched shattered Ekdal junior, Hjalmar, in photography and set him up with Gina to boot. Hjalmar, naïvely grateful, suspected no foul play by Werle with either Ekdal or Gina. Nor does he ever suspect any in retrospect despite Werle's continuing help to the insolvent ménage down the years in the form of secret subsidies to the tight household budget and overpayments to old Ekdal for copy work since his release. The play opens as Werle's estranged son, righteous Gregers, puts two and two together when he revisits his father and his old schoolmate Hjalmar like a ghost out of the past after sixteen or seventeen years spent at his father's mills and mines in the backwoods up north, out of touch with the rest of life except through perfunctory business correspondence with his father. Werle, long since widowed, has invited Gregers back home for a spell, hoping to mend their relations before marrying his current housekeeper, gracious Mrs. Sørby. Werle's grand reception of Gregers proves unavailing: Gregers rebuffs his calculated fatherly advances and moves into the Ekdals' spare room, intent on dispelling the falsity at the root of Hjalmar's marriage. This intent comes of his old friendship for Hjalmar and, backing that up, a filial malice he calls "the claim of the ideal." Tragedy ensues. Hjalmar, his eyes opened, repudiates his wife and Hedvig—irresolutely, but with such bathos that the impressionable girl sets out to propitiate him by shooting the wild duck (he has inveighed against "that junk"[2] in passing) and winds up shooting herself instead.

Of the two morals of this intense and gloomy drama, one is explicit to the point of didacticism. Its mouthpiece is Hjalmar's neighbor Relling, a doctor who helps to sustain life around him by injections of patient-specific illusions—he calls them "life-lies"[3]—while dulling the pain of his own disillusion by drink. To Gregers, in whom he diagnoses a "pesky fever of integrity,"[4] Relling tartly explains his method with reference to a dissipated divine he has made to pass for daemonic. "If I hadn't done that," he tells Gregers, "the poor harmless slob would have succumbed to self-contempt and despair years ago."[5] Relling adds that old Ekdal, the once-proud woodsman, found a comparable treatment for himself by installing a fake forest in the studio loft and filling it with rabbits and poultry that he stalks like wild game with his broken hunting rifle and in the officer's cap he is forbidden to wear outdoors. Later Hjalmar the dreamy idler, in the shock of his undeceiving about Hedvig, admits to Gregers that a great invention he has ostensibly been hatching for years in order to restore his family honor was all Relling's idea: "For God's sake, what do you expect me to invent, anyway?"[6] he asks pathetically. Until his undeceiving, Hjalmar has functioned contentedly enough by the unreality principle not just as an imaginary inventor, but as an imaginary father, photographer, family provider, and—as if only to humor old Ekdal—big-game hunter as well. Nor will this faker's genuine deep grief over Hedvig's death stay genuine beyond even a single season: as Relling puts it to Gregers, "*Then* listen to the vomit about 'the child untimely torn from its father's breast,' *then* watch him wallow in sentimentality and self-admiration and self-pity. Just you wait!"[7] Earlier, when Gregers proposes to "rescue" Hjalmar "from all the lies and deceit that threaten to destroy him," old Werle asks Gregers sardonically in Relling's own vein, "Do you think you'll be doing him a favor?"[8] Indeed, Gregers does him, and not just him, no favor in tearing that "web of deceit"[9] from the Ekdal household. By his evil touch Gregers unintentionally vindicates the life-lie as against his own spurious "claim of the ideal." Even with all his fanaticism, Gregers has stopped short of opening shattered old Ekdal's eyes about having been framed by his former logging partner—about "that time the trap was laid for Lieutenant Ekdal."[10] Nor is the life-lie in *The Wild Duck* confined to the Ekdal ménage and Relling's daemonic roommate. It extends as well to Werle cloaking his ruthlessness in grave respectability and, in the biggest way, to Gregers himself moralizing his spite against Werle. Thus Relling tells Gregers to use the plain word "lies" in lieu of "this fancy word 'ideals.' "[11] The focal life-lie in *The Wild Duck* is no less the domestic setup that centers around Hjalmar.

So is that setup the privileged conveyance for the second, subtextual moral of Ibsen's play: that the human family goes against nature. Ibsen's undercover argument is that domesticity maims and thwarts the human animal made for the wild, free life of sea and forest, just as it preserves human defectives only to debilitate and devitalize the human breed as a whole. Comparable drastic takeoffs on Darwinism were then rampant among Europe's moral radicals. Ibsen's variant differs from a Nietzsche's or even a Strindberg's primarily in looking strikingly silly when lifted aboveboard and formulated in so many words, as it is in his preparatory notes for the play. But this does not prevent his case against the home, a man's proverbial castle at that time of all times, from achieving uncanny cogency and power subrationally onstage, as an undertheme of *The Wild Duck*.

The vehicle for that undertheme, the Ekdal family at frontstage center, fast emerges as an artificial, effete contrivance supported from the wings by Hedvig's "natural" father. Little Hedvig is already half blind from a degenerative eye ailment afflicting Werle only late in life. Ekdal, in his prison cell and later in his domestic refuge, has sunk from sporting outdoorsman to doddering souse. Gina, brought low by Werle, has stayed low even as the mainstay of the "cramped and shoddy"[12] Ekdal household—untutored, servile, overtaxed, scraping along. But it is Hjalmar who steals this sickly familial show. Raised, and spoiled, by "two crackpot, hysterical maiden aunts,"[13] he has come way down from the fair-haired boy of his college class, proudly "declaiming other people's poetry and other people's ideas,"[14] to a coddled psychological cripple and a kept man once removed, prating about himself as "a bread-winner"[15]

with a lofty "mission in life."[16] Nor does Werle's first marriage redress the
domestic balance, what with his deranged wife driven to drink by his infidelities
and, in return, bending his ear with "hell-fire sermons" day and night[17] while
sickening their son's conscience over the paternal sins. "Gregers—I don't think
there's a man on earth you hate as much as me": such is Werle's epitaph on his
failed fatherhood.[18] Of Gregers, who hints that his days are numbered,[19] Ibsen
noted in his marginal jottings: "It is the family that has ruined him!"[20] The
sturdiest figure of the lot is cut by wicked Werle, his "long career" like "a
battlefield strewn at every turn with shattered lives."[21] With reference to the
frankness between Werle and Mrs. Sørby, Hjalmar observes bitterly that "it's
not I but *he* who will achieve the true marriage."[22] True or not, Werle's will be
a sterile twilight marriage to a housekeeper on the make who means to repay
her big "catch," as she puts it,[23] by tending him in his coming blindness. Her
attitude emerges most clearly from her explanation of why she had once
spurned Relling in the forest lands: "I have always been careful not to act on
impulse. After all, a woman can't afford to throw herself away."[24]

Old Ekdal alone even remotely articulates the pervasive undertheme of
domestication dragging out stunted lives against nature only to stunt them
still further in the process. Three times he delivers himself of a portentous
utterance about the forest's "revenge"—once to warn against too much felling,
and twice just after Hedvig has shot herself.[25] The dark suggestion is that
Hedvig's suicide, like his own imprisonment, was a penalty paid for violating
nature. The overtheme of the life-lie conjoins with the undertheme of the
family being counter to nature in Hjalmar's double need for fakery and family
just to survive.

Overtheme and undertheme conjoin as well, with mutual enhancement, in
a shadowy presence lurking behind the scenes: that of the wild duck. For all
its symbolic overlay, the duck is a natural component of the plot. It is
introduced during Gregers's initial, nighttime visit to the Ekdals' studio. Old
Ekdal having muttered a first time about the forest's revenge, Gregers asks how
he, a great outdoorsman, can stand to live confined by four walls in a stuffy
city. By way of reply Ekdal, overruling Hjalmar's embarrassment, insists on
Gregers's being shown the contrived hunting grounds behind sliding doors at
the rear of the stage. Then he proudly points out what he calls "the *real* thing"[26]
in that fake forest housing a menagerie barely visible by moonlight: the wild
duck in its basket. The exchanges that follow tell the duck's and, straight
through it, the Ekdals' story (the "Pettersen" mentioned being Werle's servant
already known to the audience):

EKDAL Oh, they're most remarkable, let me tell you, these wild ducks.

GREGERS But how did you ever catch it, Lieutenant Ekdal?

EKDAL Wasn't me that caught it. There's a certain man here in town we have to thank for her.

GREGERS [*struck by a thought*] That man wouldn't happen to be my father, would he?

EKDAL Oh yes indeed. Precisely your father. Hm.

HJALMAR Funny you should guess that, Gregers.

GREGERS Well, you told me before that you owed such a lot to my father, so it occurred to me that . . .

GINA But we didn't get the duck from Mr. Werle personally . . .

EKDAL It's Håkon Werle we have to thank for her just the same, Gina. *[To GREGERS.]* He was out in a boat, you see, and took a shot at her. But it happens his sight isn't so good anymore, your father's. Hm. So she was only winged.

GREGERS I see. She got some shot in her.

HJALMAR Yes, a few.

HEDVIG It was in the wing, so she couldn't fly.

GREGERS So she dived to the bottom, I suppose?

EKDAL [*sleepily, his voice thick*] Goes without saying. Always do that, wild ducks. Plunge to the bottom—as deep as they can get, old chap—bite themselves fast in the weeds and the tangle—and all the other damn mess down there. And they never come up again.

GREGERS But, Lieutenant Ekdal, *your* wild duck did come up again.

EKDAL He had such an absurdly clever dog, your father . . . And that dog—it dived after and fetched the duck up again.

GREGERS [*turning to HJALMAR*] And so you brought it here?

HJALMAR Not right away. First it was taken to your father's house. But it didn't seem to thrive there, so Pettersen was told to do away with it . . .

EKDAL [*half asleep*] Hm . . . yes, Pettersen . . . Ass . . .

HJALMAR [*lowering his voice*] That was how we got it, you see. Father knows Pettersen slightly, and when he heard all this about the wild duck, he managed to get it turned over to him.

GREGERS And now it's thriving perfectly well there in the attic.

HJALMAR Yes, incredibly well. It's got quite plump. Of course, it's been in there so long now, it's forgotten what real wild life is like. That's the whole secret.

GREGERS You're probably right, Hjalmar. Just don't ever let it catch sight of sea or sky . . .[27]

The sham woodland behind sliding doors serves as a standing reminder both of the falsity built into the Ekdals' household and of the real forest in their background and ours—Ibsen's overtheme and undertheme respectively. Similarly, the duck basketed outside of its natural element conveys not just domestic confinement but also—for, as Hedvig insists, "she's a *real* wild bird"[28]—the wild life dormant within that confinement. The unnatural forest preserves the duck's damaged life just as the unnatural household preserves the Ekdals' damaged lives. More, that unnatural forest and unnatural household denature the duck and the Ekdals even in preserving them. What evidently prompted Ibsen's choice of a captive wild duck as emblematic of both his themes, and may even have prompted his undertheme itself, was Darwin's account of "how soon the wild duck, when domesticated, loses its true character."[29]

Outside of its basket and coop the duck fits snugly into the story as one more of Werle's casualties, one more of Werle's handouts to the Ekdals, one more token of the Ekdals' fantasticality. At the same time, the duck's side story fits right *over* the Werles' and Ekdals' main story. Werle shot it sportingly, carelessly, and it fell to the bottom only to be fetched up again and then slipped to the Ekdals: this renders, dreamlike, Werle's forcing sex on Gina, then palming her off on Hjalmar, even unto the little animal fished out of deep waters signifying Hedvig's birth. Hjalmar calls the duck "the damaged trophy of Mr. Werle's sport" in express reference to the Ekdals, wounded each and all by Werle.[30] Thus old Ekdal, already at one with the duck as "a lover of the great outdoors" now "shut in . . . by four walls,"[31] rejoins the duck additionally as a casualty of Werle's, the first one of the series shown on stage. Werle himself draws the connection with respect to old Ekdal's imprisonment as he tells Gregers even before the duck is introduced: "When Ekdal was released he was a broken man, altogether beyond help," adding: "There are people in this world who sink to the bottom the minute they get a couple of slugs in them, and they never come up again."[32] Similarly, Gregers sees Hjalmar as having "sunk down to the depths"[33] after Ekdal's ruination and having then remained mired "in the weeds and the tangle in the mud,"[34] meaning his marriage trap. Werle's violence done to the duck was almost literally the same as his violence done to Gina: "She got some shot in her." Hedvig's damage from Werle on a par with the duck's is that to her eyes—a less graphic equivalence except that Werle's bad eyes were why he maimed the duck in the first place. For the rest, Ibsen drew the parallel with Hedvig the most closely, pursuant to his laconic preparatory note for the play: "Hedvig like the wild duck."[35] Hedvig's damaged eyes keep her out of school, so that "she's completely cut off from her own kind"—this being what she herself says of the duck.[36] She is only the more drawn to the attic room containing, besides the forest décor, mementos of a vanished old sea captain nicknamed the Flying Dutchman after that legendary restless dead mariner: they include a travel book having as its frontispiece "a picture of Death with an hourglass, and a girl."[37] As if to mark her felt kinship with the wounded duck in its death dive, Hedvig tells Gregers that the whole attic together with everything in it always seems to her to be really and truly "the depths of the sea."[38]

That felt kinship lays the ground for the dramatic climax in all its ambiguity. Gregers has suggested to Hedvig that to regain Hjalmar's love, she try sacrificing the wild duck or, as he rephrases it to her for emphasis, "the most precious thing you have in the world."[39] She slips into the back loft, saying softly to herself: "The wild duck!"[40] She then shoots not the duck, though, but herself, and this just when Hjalmar scoffs at the idea that she could ever give her life for him: at any such suggestion "you'd soon hear the answer I'd get!" he declares,[41] whereupon her pistol goes off. Is this Greek-style dramatic irony, or has Hedvig overheard Hjalmar? Either way, Hedvig substitutes herself for the duck, and on her birthday at that, in what she feels to be the depths of the sea. Driving the point home, Gregers exclaims grandiloquently upon her death: "In the depths of the sea . . ."[42] Old Ekdal, when condemned, had taken a pistol to himself but then, in Hjalmar's hollow words, "lost his nerve."[43] Hjalmar next had pointed that same pistol at his own breast, but, to quote him against himself again: "In the decisive moment I won the victory over myself."[44] Hedvig in turn, fulfilling the duck's bungled fate, shoots herself with that selfsame pistol in the very way that Ekdal has told her a wild duck is properly shot: "just below the breast."[45]

It is high time to schematize. Ibsen's overtheme is that life-lies are endemic to domesticated human existence: without them it would be intolerable. Its very need for lies to make it tolerable argues that domesticated human existence is against nature—Ibsen's undertheme. Overtheme and undertheme connect this way at the logical edges. Practically, though, they clash head-on in that the overtheme calls for preserving the Ekdal family for its maimed members' sake while the undertheme asks to destroy it for the maimed species' sake. In the undertheme, domesticity is against nature, or artificial, with the twofold implication that it is at once false and degenerative. In Ibsen's scheme, be it noted, nature is no mere theoretical construct or outlying rustic realm, as it had been for earlier critics of cultural artifice; rather, it is a primitive instinctual residue persisting beneath the cultivated human surface, ever ready to resurface with a vengeance, as it does in Hedvig at the climax. It is above all to protect Hedvig that Relling defends the Ekdals' family lie against Gregers. But Hedvig's suicide when that lie collapses only actualizes a deeper, stronger natural will within her, as if she were remembering "what real wild life is like."[46] In this perspective domestication, being against nature, is a "risky business," like felling trees in the forest: "You don't get away with it. The forest takes revenge."[47]

In this undertheme the nature that is repudiated within domestication is a vast stretch of human history and prehistory persisting within the present. The past persisting within the present, prone to reactivation, is tangible on stage in the Ekdals' attic with its pastist paraphernalia alluring Hedvig, including a stopped old clock: "So time has stopped in there—in the wild duck's domain," remarks Gregers, who dotes on symbols.[48] That persistence is ubiquitous, if intangible, in the dramatic structure of the play dominated by its preplay—in the highly Ibsenite preponderance of past doings over present doings. Not only has far more of the play happened before the curtain rises than happens after, and not only does their prehistory coerce the characters onstage; the whole intricate forestory is told in the course of that onstage story without ever slowing it down—an expository tour de force that immeasurably heightens the induced sense of an active, even coercive, presence of the past.

The Wild Duck is a triumph over the many implausibilities that come into it. Some even belong to it. One of the first and worst of these is how very naïve Hjalmar must be never to have doubted his paternity of Hedvig after Werle sloughed off Gina on him precisely because she was pregnant. This naïveté is of a piece with his inveterate wishful thinking, as when he, a would-be great inventor, dozes beside his scientific journals, their pages uncut. Ibsen did regularly go the limit, or even beyond it, in approaching the everyday—in this case fooling oneself as a way of life—through the extreme rather than the mean. This approach was common in his time. In fiction he shared it with the naturalists as against their forerunners, the realists. He shared it also with a Durkheim exploring social normalcy through social pathology and a Freud exploring human normalcy through human pathology. Integral to Ibsen's stagecraft was sensing (to swipe a bon mot from Jean Cocteau) how far he could go too far. Ibsen's sharpest detractor calls Werle's setting up Hjalmar with pregnant Gina implausible, but concedes: "These events may pass well enough as credible at a performance, when there is no time to consider them."[49] Just so: their incredibility blends into the play in roughly the same way that, under a master's hand, anatomical disproportions may blend into a figure painting, or painterly blotches into its texture. The measure of Ibsen's mastery in *The Wild Duck* is how great the incredibilities are that do pass at a performance to amplify the themes that carry the play.

Other implausibilities of a kind with Hjalmar's too-too gullibility abound, starting already in the powerful first act. The power of this act derives from a tension that builds up between foreground and background as Werle's ostensible breeding and propriety at a munificent dinner party he is hosting (flanked by his decorous housekeeper backed by a liveried domestic assisted by a hired waiter) emerge as a front for a callous rapacity that has victimized those closest to him. The same tension builds up concurrently between the festive occasion of his impending remarriage and the bad blood toward him that boils over in his estranged son, summoned for "a show of family life" or of "home-sweet-home."[50] Werle's fine and proper front is his life-lie, and that bad blood is Gregers's familial heritage—the overtheme and the undertheme respectively, which then carry over together to the Ekdals' studio for amplified development. To be sure, it is implausible even for Gregers, a man possessed, to have been out of touch with "my best, my only friend"[51] for sixteen or seventeen years as the curtain rises and then to persecute his best and only friend inhumanely with a claim of the ideal until the curtain falls on disaster. No doubt, but no matter. For in this dialectical play of ideas, or *pièce à double thèse*, the themes that commandeer the characters call for a Gregers returning from the backwoods for act one with a mission to destroy others' life-lies in the name of his own. Still less motivated than Gregers's retreat nearly two decades long or his "severe case of inflamed integrity"[52] is Gregers's scheme of propitiatory sacrifice that triggers the tragedy proper. Again, no matter. For in this social drama, motivation is subordinated to interaction, itself dominated by those two themes of, first, the life-lie torn away from Hjalmar only to begin forming back again around him and, second, of the family violating nature until nature finally reclaims its own.

These two morals of the play are of necessity an overtheme and an undertheme respectively: Ibsen had no leeway there. That we live by lies (or their near synonyms: deception, pretense, ideals) is, for all its brevity, too complex a proposition to be conveyed subtextually and to work the way an undertheme works, unconsciously, like the symbolism in *The Wild Duck*. Besides, it could hardly compel assent in our hearts of hearts, being nothing we all suspect deep down. As an overtheme, conversely, it may not even have needed Relling to drive it home in so many words, Greek-chorus-like, since it speaks straight out of the action. Without Relling's resounding generalized pronouncement "Take away the life-lie from the average person, and you take his happiness along with it,"[53] Ibsen's public could have missed his point no further than to question whether the Ekdals' dependency on illusion were not just their own special family foible. But even that pronouncement of Relling's leaves room for dispute whether Werle for one might not be above average or illusion-proof, hypocrisy and all. Hjalmar's steep decline from campus idol to pampered idler raises the bigger question whether the life-lie does not simply destroy some lives more slowly than does truth in the raw. The life-lie argument is no less just what a good overtheme should be: engaging, challenging, even provocative, whether right or wrong. On the other hand, we do all harbor, as a legacy of our earliest individual socializing if not of the domestication of our species, a deep-seated instinctual resentment of familial constraints such that the family ethos requires immense public pressure both legal and moral for its enforcement. Not that Ibsen's undertheme is arguable the way an overtheme is. The human animal does form families, so its families are natural after all. More, if humans do, like wild ducks, lose their true character when domesticated, they also live longer, healthier, and—by their own acquired standards—happier lives in consequence despite that inner sense of loss to which Ibsen appealed. But again, an undertheme's business is not to persuade, but to resonate.

By way of doing its business, Ibsen's undertheme in *The Wild Duck* impinges as much on the form as on the plot of the play. Its dominant form is a naturalism unaffected at any point by the symbolism surrounding the wild duck. That symbolism comes into the overtheme only peripherally and expendably even though the winged duck is the centerpiece of old Ekdal's life-lie—of his false forest primeval that yet vicariously wreaks "the forest's revenge." Yet that symbolism amounts to a second form in that it bears nearly the whole burden of expressing an undertheme conveyed outright by little else in the play, and then only darkly as by the family's secret support from Hedvig's "natural" father. Except for that symbolism, the Ekdal family could be seen as protective rather than degenerative, and the Werles as just a *famille manquée*, as when Gregers asks his father: "When was there ever any family life around here?"[54] It is the wild duck that creates the polarity of wild versus domesticated with, at the domestic pole, the connotations of tamed, wounded, and degenerate. The undertheme feeds into the plot in that Hedvig's suicide would come across as a contrived outrage rather than a tragic fulfillment without her felt affinity for that duck that took the plunge. Gina may be objectively admirable, but Hedvig alone is moving, her infirmity aiding, so that we ought to feel partial to her life-lying family insofar as she loves and needs it. But Ibsen's undertheme, mediated by his symbolical duck, makes of that love and need a dire comedown. Only with this subtextual reason behind it does Hedvig's ill-motivated suicide work. And then it works spectacularly.

NOTES

1. *Ibsen*, trans. and ed. James Walter McFarlane (London: Oxford University Press, 1960), vol. 6, 430. This volume will be cited as "Oxford"; "Ibsen" will refer to Henrik Ibsen, *The Wild Duck*, trans. and ed. Dounia B. Christiani (New York: Norton, 1968).

2. Ibsen, 48.

3. Ibid., 63.

  4. Ibid., 63; cf. 46.
  5. Ibid., 64.
  6. Ibid., 69.
  7. Ibid., 74.
  8. Ibid., 45.
  9. Ibid., 50.
 10. Ibid., 45.
 11. Ibid., 64.
 12. Ibid., 23.
 13. Ibid., 62.
 14. Ibid., 63.
 15. Ibid., 41.
 16. Ibid., 30, also 39.
 17. Ibid., 54.
 18. Ibid., 15.
 19. Ibid., 45.
 20. Oxford, 435.
 21. Ibsen, 15.
 22. Ibid., 56.
 23. Ibid., 54.
 24. Ibid.
 25. Ibid., 25, 72, 73.
 26. Ibid., 27.
 27. Ibid., 27–28 (suspension points all Ibsen's).
 28. Ibid., 36.
 29. Ibid., 149.
 30. Ibid., 52.
 31. Ibid., 26.
 32. Ibid., 12.
 33. Ibid., 41.
 34. Ibid., 29.
 35. Oxford, 434.
 36. Ibsen, 36.
 37. Ibid., 35.
 38. Ibid., 36.
 39. Ibid., 60.
 40. Ibid., 67.
 41. Ibid., 71.
 42. Ibid., 73 (Ibsen's suspension points).
 43. Ibid., 39.
 44. Ibid., 40.
 45. Ibid., 65.
 46. Ibid., 28.

47. Ibid., 25.

48. Ibid., 35.

49. Ronald Gray, *Ibsen—a dissenting view: A study of the last twelve plays* (Cambridge: Cambridge University Press, 1977), 100.

50. Ibsen, 15.

51. Ibid., 5.

52. Ibid., 46.

53. Ibid., 64.

54. Ibid., 15.

13

Death Beckoning
Thomas Mann's *Death in Venice*

The story line of Thomas Mann's 1912 novella *Death in Venice* is short and straight. An aging author settled in Munich travels south on an impulse for a brief respite from his harsh and lonely literary labors, finds his way as if by enchantment to Venice in all its moldy magnificence, and there is secretly so smitten with a Polish boy among the other guests summering in the same grand hotel on the Lido that he cannot tear himself away despite a spreading plague to which he eventually succumbs. The narrative, richly and finely wrought, often verges on a studied monologue by the solitary, self-enclosed hero as it recounts his fatal escapade from his own perspective, tracking his furtive thoughts and feelings through their innermost twists and turns. Only rarely does it back away far enough to reflect on his fate with a detachment beyond his own reach. That fate is of his own making in all its essentials even after he lets himself go—even after he relaxes his strenuous, disciplined grip on life once he has avowed his forbidden love to himself. At this point his virile moralism starts yielding irreversibly to a reckless effeminate lust that wells up from his depths and that he recognizes in the process as the great source from which his artistry had drawn its secret sustenance all along. Because Mann's hapless hero—Gustav Aschenbach, latterly *von* Aschenbach—is presented straight off as a figure of European culture at its height, the message *en clair* is that culture, being grounded in repression, carries with it a standing risk of regression such that, paradoxically, creativity at its loftiest is prone to self-destruct.

Before his sentimental misadventure in Venice, creativity in this authoritative author is both released and policed with a perfervid, consuming sense of purpose. A scion of sober, dedicated Prussian state servants on his father's side, Aschenbach strives to subject his art to a rule of law as strict and firm as that imposed on his ancestral realm by its warrior kings. Day after day he rises before dawn to a strenuous, austere regimen of wresting phrases from forced imaginings, wrenching them into literary shape, and impressing upon them a look of spontaneity as of a single outpouring. Behind its smooth and stately front his consummately crafted prose is built up bit by bit out of disparate, minute, fugitive stirrings of the heart fastened upon, nailed down, and joined together into finished works that are so many triumphant, if increasingly joyless, concealments of a growing weariness. These finished works themselves, as befits their begetting, uphold a stern ethic of tireless perseverance, of scorn for laxity or self-pity in whatever guise, of contempt for the foibles to which the flesh is heir. Flouting his own frail health, Mann's prophet of steadfastness against all odds and defiance of every limitation is himself the very model of the suffering-active virtue and the heroism of weakness that his writings extol. His style at length officialized and his person ennobled, Aschenbach toils on only the more titanically at his desk as at a lonely outpost. Achieving literary mastery and personal dignity only by a continual laborious overcoming, administering his hard-won renown like a conquered province, straining and at length overstraining to fulfill "the tasks laid upon him by his ego and the European soul,"[1] declining all facility, repudiating all sensuality, concealing all signs of inner wear and tear, he is living beyond his moral means, with nerves taut and teeth clenched. In so doing, he is leading the dangerous life of the artist as a "born deceiver."[2] For behind that tireless travail his art is a covert fantasy indulgence, his labor of letters a sensual-aesthetic exercise, and his fame an unconscious aphrodisiac.

At those perilous heights of repression, such a supreme *Kulturmensch* is just that supremely vulnerable to regression. And regress Aschenbach does, little by little, through the whole course of the tale. Indeed, he regresses on two levels at once: cultural and erotic. Culturally he is in vibrant rapport with his own times as the action begins, speaking straight to the hearts of a vast youthful readership thankful to him for his recent novelistic celebration of all those who, overburdened, labor at the edge of exhaustion for a worthy life or even a touch of greatness. Looking backward, he is proud of his early essay on aesthetics that readers ranked with one by Schiller, proud of the crisp exchanges between Voltaire and Frederick the Great in his epic novel set in the Seven Years War, proud of his acquired purity of language such as Louis XIV is said to have prescribed for himself—proud, in sum, of his closeness to the spirit and style of the great modern standard-setters. As soon as he starts to relax, his musings drift through snatches of Goethe and August von Platen on their way back to high classicism. Then, on reaching the Lido, he recurs instead in his literary fancy to Virgil and Plutarch, to Xenophon, Socrates, and Homer; once his idle thoughts even slip into Homeric hexameters as he mentally casts his daily doings and observations in Greek mythic molds. He blesses the comely Polish lad, Tadzio, Christianly early along, then paganizes him in flights of fancy, only to awake one morning in a cold sweat from a dream of an archaic phallic procession celebrating his ephebic idol in place of the tempter god Dionysus.

Erotically, meanwhile, his point of departure is a homosexuality buried in his discipleship of Frederick the Great and in his self-identification with Saint Sebastian. Even buried, it brings on a fateful fit of restlessness when, still in Munich, he merely glimpses a bold, southern-looking male vagabond. On shipboard along his way south he advances through a fascinated distaste for a senile fop (who prefigures his own comedown) to a felt kinship with gay August von Platen as he reaches his bewitching final destination. Then, as he settles into the watery wonderland, he graduates to an inhibited attraction for Tadzio that revives old thoughts about beauty as the one pure idea to appear sensually and old erotic fancies drained in his abstemious life's service. He sinks into pedophile voyeurism while watching the divinized youngster sea-bathe. Later he also sneaks along after the Polish party on its jaunts through sinuous canals and jagged alleyways, ogling Tadzio with a passion that ultimately enslaves his soul in the course of that dream of a savage sexual free-for-all in the godlike youngster's train. With this final instinctual upsurge, all the base cravings that Aschenbach's lifelong literary toil had served to dam up or work up turn against his embattled ordering ego with a voluptuous vengeance, shaming him in his shattered remnants of ancestral pride while destroying "his whole life's culture"[3] overnight. His whole life's culture that succumbs is likewise the culture of Europe's lifetime, as if in a giganticized replay of Thebes succumbing to the divine madness brought to it from the Orient by Dionysus and his celebrants.

Closer in scale than lone Aschenbach to Thebes subverted by an epidemic frenzy from the Orient is Venice undermined by a deadly plague from the Orient that spawns crime and vice while festering under official denial and repression conjoined. Aschenbach sniffs out that worsening pestilence and, once he has acknowledged it to himself over his initial resistance, rejoices in its progress, keeping an eager watch over "the foul undercover goings-on in Venice, that adventure of the world outside him which darkly joined with the one in his heart to feed his passion with vague, lawless hopes."[4] Plagued Venice thus takes on the very aspect of Aschenbach's sick psyche. To him in his illicit pursuit as also to Venetian lowlife, "every rent in the civic fabric will be welcome."[5] He thrills at seeing through the official coverup of "that evil secret of the city's which fused with his own and which it meant so much for him to keep"[6]—this lest the vacationing Polish party pack up and off, to be sure, but even more by the force of that very fusion. Sanitation and law enforcement are undermined as the public authorities make common cause with local hotel keepers, merchants, and even criminals to keep the dirty secret under wraps so as not to lose the tourist trade. This corruption on high encourages the baser elements of the populace to act out their "dark antisocial drives" unabashedly and unrestrainedly.[7] To Aschenbach's "somber satisfaction,"[8] the city's collusion with its underworld proves its undoing as license and lawlessness run rampant along its fetid byways and up its nasty back alleys.

Mann pushes this pointed parallel between Aschenbach and Venice well beyond even these morbid parameters. Just like Aschenbach's artistry at once moralizing and demoralizing, Venice is a tricky, two-faced thing—half land and half sea, "half fairy tale, half tourist trap."[9] Just like Aschenbach's art inspired from dubious depths, Venice is a portal to Europe for irrational, plague-fomenting regions beyond Europe's pale where the vices now surfacing along the lagoon are at home. Just like Aschenbach the titled artist slipping over the brink, Venice too is a "sunken queen" in its decaying splendor, a cultural monument being sapped from below out of filthy canals and through moldy, crumbling walls. As Aschenbach, exhausted one sultry day from his latest chase after Tadzio, eats a handful of overripe strawberries, his eye is caught by a grand façade with a void behind it where once a palazzo had been. This image throws back to the opening theme of the tale, that of Aschenbach's art concealing his inner depletion—a theme expressed even at that starting point in such physical terms as "the elegant self-mastery eaten away by a biological decay that it hides from the world's eyes to the very last: the yellow ugliness that, though a sensual handicap, can yet kindle its seething ardor to pure flame, goading itself on to supremacy in the very realm of beauty."[10] In return, these physical terms anticipate Aschenbach's last fling, when the burnt-out artist who had looked ahead to an old age with a full life's experience behind it for his art to draw upon turns into a death-ridden degenerate cosmetically rejuvenating himself, artificially masking an exhaustion previously overwritten by the contrived sprightliness of his prose.

Death stalks Aschenbach as if outwardly throughout the tale before closing in on him for the kill. In the text proper, with its explicit theme of the revenge of the repressed, death is no more or less than the wages of his reckless passion. The subtext, however, extends that overt theme so that Aschenbach acts out his fate instead of simply meeting it in an unguarded moment through those mushy strawberries. He is a suicide, as Mann called him in a preparatory note for the novella,[11] only not from shame or despair or disenchantment like the usual suicides of earlier fiction. Rather, death is the end term of his regression, the undertow of his flood of instinctual release.[12] Nor is his suicidal course presented as special pathology. His only special pathology is the one stressed at the outset, when it is shown at its apogee: the all-too-high level of repression set by his cultural aspirations on top of his sexual self-denial. Once the psychic lid lifts, his tabooed erotism overflows, unloosing a deadly thrust at its core that it normally absorbs—a deeper striving for an end of all striving, for a primal peace without duty or desire. Death is at the end of Aschenbach's regressive line, at the base of his instinctual pit—and not just of his alone, for such fundamentals are not meant to vary from one individual to the next. Here, then, in Mann's subtext, is a clearcut conception of sexuality as a derivative and overlay of a basic, universal death drive, and of culture in turn as a derivative and overlay of the sex drive. It belongs to this subtext of Mann's on a par with his text that culture is the more tenuous the higher it is pitched.

This subtext is inseparable from Mann's expressionistic narrative scheme. Expressionism proper distorts physical reality to reflect an artist's own or a central character's intense experience of it. *Death in Venice*, while it stops short of full-fledged expressionism, does manipulate physical reality to reflect Aschenbach's subjective needs and train of thought, and this to the very last in Aschenbach's own most cultivated literary idiom. Thus the weather projects his mood, actual or impending. Thus too the other characters and their doings appear as emanations of his psyche,[13] actualizing his inner purposes. Chance itself obeys his secret will: when he would sensibly cut short his stay in Venice but cannot bear to leave Tadzio, his trunk is misdirected so that he can delay his departure unintentionally. Even the plague respects his schedule: he succumbs punctually just as the Poles are packed to leave. In line with his outer story unfolding as if from within him, he is solitary and mute from first to last except for conventional, impersonal contacts and phrases. The narrative points up his withdrawal and self-enclosure by styling him "the loner," "the mute one"—"der Einsame," "der Stumme," once even "der Einsam-Stumme." He exchanges no words and few glances with Tadzio in particular, who remains unintelligible in his own right unless as a pubescent Narcissus adoring himself in his lover's furtive, fevered gaze. The narrative is aligned with the hero's own perspective even where it comes short by design, as when it evokes his brief, happy marriage in his youth through a single, cursory, vitalike phrase fit for an obituary. This expressionistic narrative mode was not alone Mann's at the time; a far more flagrant use of it in the same year as *Death in Venice*, 1912, was Franz

Kafka's in *The Metamorphosis*, which recounts from its hero's own vantage point his delusion of having turned into a bug.[14] Unlike Kafka's hero, Mann's has no need to hallucinate, as reality meets all his unspoken wants.

Also expressionistically, symbols that cross Aschenbach's path link up in the narrative with others that cross his mind. The opening passage finds him thoughtlessly reading tombstone inscriptions at a stonecutter's opposite a mortuary chapel. Next his gaze alights on a skeletal, exotic vagabond who, standing in the Grecian archway of the chapel, glares boldly back at him and then vanishes. Of an instant he pictures to himself a rank primeval jungle with a fierce tiger crouching, its eyes aglow. Then already, "his heart pounding from terror and enigmatic longing,"[15] his decision is taken to journey far away, as if in a dream of death.[16] Much later he associates back to that funerary chapel and that vagabond when a travel clerk confirms his suspicion that a plague has struck Venice. That figure of death from the chapel portico (a derivative of the "bone man" spawned by the bubonic plague and long familiar in art and letters) reappears as the gay old dandy on Aschenbach's Adriatic steamer, then as his exotic, shady, Charon-like gondolier, and again in his hotel courtyard in the guise of a balladmonger stinking of disinfectant: all four of them intrigue and repel him at once. The rank jungle in his vision prompted by the bold, bony, southerly stranger recurs in the travel clerk's account of the plague having germinated in the Ganges delta. The fresh strawberries that he enjoys while first watching Tadzio on the beach reappear soggy, rotten, and deadly on the very spot where he had once resolved to flee Venice. The laughter pealed out by the quarantined singing buffoon in his hotel garden reechoes as Tadzio's lilting name intoned in the lewd frenzy of his devastating Dionysian dream. The hour glass that, early in the tale, images his fear of dying before his life's work is done comes back to haunt his musings just when the south Italian buffoon's act is over. This redoubling, tripling, or quadrupling across time of suggestive elements of the hero's experience, whether outer or inner, lends that stream of experience a semblance of fatedness, as if it were all continually subject to a single will. To this same effect of his pursuit of an inner purpose unknown to him, and with a bonus of irony, Aschenbach searches his heart on approaching Venice whether some "late-life sentimental adventure"[17] might not await him there. "A strange expansion of what was inside him"[18] is how the narrator describes Aschenbach's reaction to the skeletal vagabond vanishing, meaning only a sudden restlessness but suggesting the correspondence between his innermost longings and the contingencies of his incipient quest for escape.

Within this "strange expansion" of what is inside him Aschenbach's thoughts tend to death continually: as he gazes out from his ship deck onto infinite, empty horizons; as he nestles into the coffin-black seat of a coffin-black gondola reminiscent of "death itself,"[19] wishing the ride might last forever, with Charon incarnate rowing; as in his beach chair he ponders the weary artist's love for the sea as nothingness or else daydreams timelessly about simply dissolving; as he rejoices at the sight of Tadzio's brittle teeth or again at the sound of Tadzio's hard breathing, each betokening an early death; as he holds with August von Platen that to have looked on beauty is to be slated for death; and so on and on, with decadent, death-infested Venice soon amplifying the theme at every turn. Indeed, the strangest "strange expansion" outwards of what is inside him is his fellowship with the stricken city denying the death within it—denying that titular "death in Venice" that sparks indefinable hopes of "frightful sweetness"[20] in him.

Earlier I likened Aschenbach's resolve to travel, after his glimpse of a mysterious stranger and his flash of a tiger crouching, to a dream of death. The same likeness holds for Aschenbach's outer story unfolding symbol-laden out of his innermost will: this expressionistic narrative mode resembles nothing so much as dreaming. Strindberg maintained in a 1908 preface to *A Dream Play* of 1902 that his whole expressionist theater was modeled on dreams. Mann's narrative itself insists repeatedly in *Death in Venice* how dreamy the consciousness is that it conveys, and this alike whether it is recording inner or outer reality. The sight of the bony vagabond before the chapel in Munich draws Aschenbach out of his "daydreams."[21] On first observing the old coxcomb on shipboard, Aschenbach feels "as if the world were starting to settle into a dreamlike strangeness, a weird distortion"[22]; on seeing that same creepy, coquettish old codger a couple of pages later, Aschenbach feels once again as if the world were turning "dizzily bizarre and grotesque"[23]; in between, before he dozes off, that oldster and a hunchbacked ticket clerk flit through Aschenbach's mind with "confused dream words."[24] On nearing Venice, Aschenbach runs through some measured lyrics of "the sorrowful and ardent poet the turrets and towers of whose dreams had once risen from those waters to meet him,"[25] this lyrical dreamer being gay Platen again, here coyly unnamed. On his first gondola ride to the Lido as if across the Styx, it strikes Aschenbach "dreamily"[26] that his oarsman might be a cutthroat. His exhilarating cogitations about beauty when he first sees Tadzio at dinner promptly seem to Aschenbach shallow, like "intimations from a dream,"[27] and he goes off to a night's sleep full of real "dream images."[28] As he sits on the beach the next day, he is "dreaming . . . deeply into the void"[29] just when Tadzio walks by. His trunk going astray is a "comically dreamlike adventure,"[30] and he rests up for a good hour afterwards, "thoughtlessly dreaming."[31] Resuming his routine, he sits on the beach mornings "dreaming out over the azure sea"[32] even as his beloved often dreams "into the blue."[33] He rises early, while the sea still lies "blinding white in morning dreams"[34] or even before, to dream himself back to sleep while awaiting the dawn with Tadzio's name on his lips.[35] Later in the day "his heart would dream tender fancies."[36] Whenever Tadzio is out of sight, he wants only "to dream of him."[37] During the balladmonger's act the laughter and carbolic stench together with Tadzio's nearness cast a "dream spell"[38] over him. He "dreams" an instant of alerting Tadzio's mother to the plague.[39] He leaves his cosmetician's parlor "dream-happy."[40] He soliloquizes in "weird dream logic"[41] as he eats his terminal strawberries. At every step of his way he seems to be sleepwalking. In his fateful, "fearful dream"[42] of the tempter god's lewd rites he gradually turns into the wild celebrants that he begins by watching— and so indeed is his waking relation to his surroundings a self-relation. Erasing what remains of the line between dream and reality, the narrative questions whether that dire Dionysian nighttime event can properly be termed a dream at all, and again later whether his anxious feeling of "issuelessness"[43] refers to himself or to the world outside as he walks to his beach chair one last time.

Aschenbach's premonition of his death and his headlong rush to meet it emerge, then, from Mann's text only by implication. They emerge time and again through the symbolic value of his wandering thoughts together with— thanks to the dreamlike narrative technique—the omens that cross his path. In fact, both the logic and the suggestive force of that technique make his death, like everything else in the tale, into his own doing. More, either pole of his lifelong tension between repression and release, control and uncontrol, is deathlike: cold formalism on the one side and hot dissolution on the other. His affinity for death is most nearly explicit in his remaining in Venice knowing of the plague, his feeling that he could not survive his imminent separation from Tadzio, and his eating those high-risk strawberries as his time nears its end. Never, though, does Aschenbach or his narrator recognize outright, in so many words, that in chasing after Tadzio he is really chasing after death. In his fateful phallic dream the promiscuous revelers do feast on each other's flesh and blood as part of the fun besides fusing with the dreamer before their orgy is done: their divine rapture puts them, and hence him, at mortal risk. But death is not the orgiasts' aim despite that gory hint of it. Through that devastating dream, therefore, Aschenbach's self-concealments lift just short of his death wish. Mann supplies the omission not only by matching Aschenbach's objective experience that issues in death with his fantasy world within, but vicariously too for good measure by having him see his own likeness in afflicted Venice, feel an affinity for the death on the loose there, join the sick city in its coverup, go giddy with joy as this "complicity" opens up obscure vistas of "chaos,"[44] and take a "bizarre satisfaction"[45] in goading knowing Venetians into outright lies about the death on the loose in their midst. As a clincher, Aschenbach literalizes the implied equivalence between the death wish within him and the death plaguing Venice around him when he succumbs to the city's sickness. Besides suffusing the text in these multiple ways, the subtext extends it logically: Aschenbach is still regressing in dying. No wonder readers tend to imagine that Aschenbach's death wish is right up there in simple affirmation on the textual surface of the tale.

If Aschenbach does not recognize death, that consummate, eternal release from duty and desire, as the ultimate goal of his frenetic escapade, that is because in Mann's conception this final sense of it can never be grasped through introspection, from which Aschenbach shies away in any case for all his inwardness. As Freud, its later theorist, was to argue, the death drive works in concealment, never manifesting unalloyed,[46] so that it can be known only inferentially apart from its frightful and enticing mythic-symbolic showings. Enticing is Tadzio in a mythic-symbolic posture, seeming to beckon from the end of a sand bar against the horizon as Aschenbach watches from his beach chair in his last throes before rising to join him. And frightful is the war scare that hangs over Europe as the tale opens, whereupon the narrative focus narrows to Aschenbach for the duration before abruptly spreading back out worldwide at the very close.

NOTES

1. Thomas Mann, *Die Erzählungen*, vol. 1 (Frankfurt/Main: Fischer, 1967), 340.

2. Ibid., 345.

3. Ibid., 393.

4. Ibid., 384.

5. Ibid., 381.

6. Ibid.

7. Ibid., 391.

8. Ibid., 381.

9. Ibid., 383.

10. Ibid., 345.

11. Manfred Dierks, *Studien zu Mythos und Psychologie bei Thomas Mann: An seinem Nachlass orientierte Untersuchungen zum "Tod in Venedig", zum "Zauberberg" und zur "Joseph"-Tetralogie* (Bern: Francke, 1972), 21.

12. Cf. Arnold Hirsch, *Der Gattungsbegriff "Novelle"* (Berlin: Emil Ebering, 1928), 139, 140, 143.

13. Cf. ibid., 140.

14. Cf. my "What *The Metamorphosis* Means," in *Soundings* (New York: Psychohistory Press, 1981), 7–14.

15. Mann, 340.

16. Cf. Hirsch, 143.

17. Mann, 351.

18. Ibid., 340 ("eine seltsame Ausweitung seines Innern").

19. Ibid., 353.

20. Ibid., 392; cf. Charles Baudelaire, "Les deux bonnes soeurs," in *Oeuvres complètes*, ed. Yves-Gérard le Dantec (Paris: Pléiade, 1954), 185 ("d'affreuses douceurs" link alcove and coffin).

21. Mann, 339 ("Träumereien").

22. Ibid., 350.

23. Ibid., 352.

24. Ibid., 351.

25. Ibid.

26. Ibid., 354.

27. Ibid., 359.

28. Ibid.

29. Ibid., 362.

30. Ibid., 369.

31. Ibid.

32. Ibid., 371.

33. Ibid., 373.

34. Ibid., 371.

35. Ibid., 377.

36. Ibid.

37. Ibid., 383.

38. Ibid., 388.

39. Ibid., 392.

40. Ibid., 395.

41. Ibid., 397.

42. Ibid., 392.

43. Ibid., 398.

44. Ibid., 392.

45. Ibid., 384.

46. But for Freud as against Mann, the death drive down in the depths of life was no derivative of Eros. Mann's conception more nearly paralleled the one propounded also in 1911–1912 by Sabina Spielrein; see my "Vom Sterben betrunken: Sigmund Freud als Kulturerscheinung seiner Zeit," *Inn* 11, no. 32 (May 1994): 17–23.

14

From Plagued Thebes to Plagued Venice

The monographic portion of this study of text and subtext in classic fiction has closed none too early in literary history. For the more recent a work included, the riskier its inclusion. Classics are notoriously hard to identify at close range: some works esteemed on a par with Shakespeare's or Goethe's in their day are laughable in ours. So Mann's work may yet lose its magic. His *Death in Venice* is perhaps the more vulnerable in that Aschenbach's fatal foible fell in with an eroticization of death that began with the romantics (*Werther* pointed ahead to it) but that has fairly run its course by now even along the pop trail of comic strips, rock lyrics, and movie thrillers.

The death wish in Mann's subtext rationalizes the very gloom it casts over the tale. For Aschenbach only gets what he wants in the end insofar as he has been stalking his death all along, albeit unwittingly. Not just deathly *Death in Venice*, but all twelve classics that I have analyzed here are rife with sorrow. This was not my preference. Classics run that way, with jollity the happy exception. But as in *Death in Venice*, so in my other eleven specimens, whatever goes wrong in them textually is right subtextually, though no less painful to the protagonists. After all, Sophocles' Oedipus was hell-bent on reliving his constitutive trauma. So was Matthew's Jesus heaven-bent on expiating his "innocent crime." Thomas's and Gottfried's Tristan, in dying, fulfilled his "hereditary love" for Isolde. Similarly, Francesca's eternal plight is her own lusty choice, nor is the world they lose a fit place for a Lear or a Cordelia anyway. Racine's subtext spreads Phaedra's guilt to all humankind, and Goethe's vindicates his Werther's suicide. Subtextually Julien's execution is inescapable no matter what, just as Félicité's pathetic existence is our common lot at bottom. The flawed creation that Dostoyevsky's Inquisitor throws up to Christ is nobody's fault, and the plunge that Hedvig takes is only natural. Here, then, is a first shared tendency of our twelve subtexts: to rationalize the sorrows in the texts even if they stay just as sorrowful.

Was this rationalizing intentional on the authors' parts? In no case did I yet consider directly whether the twelve subtexts I have teased out of concealment were planted deliberately. Notations by Ibsen and Mann indicate that at least those for *The Wild Duck* and *Death in Venice* were. Flaubert's recorded references to "A Simple Heart" and Dostoyevsky's drafts for "The Grand Inquisitor" point that same way. So, circumstantially, does Goethe's conscious ambivalence toward his Werther ever after seeing him into print and Racine's having openly repented his womanizing once he produced *Phaedra*. Ditto Dante: although his Francesca poses as an ingénue swept away with her timid reading partner by a naughty French romance, real-life Francesca was, he knew, the mother of an eight-year-old and her clandestine partner a father three times over. Besides, the very fact that the subtexts are all of a thematic kind with the text itself suggests that they were all thought out.

Only for *Werther* and, in lesser measure, "The Grand Inquisitor" have I considered the authors' personal stakes in their subtexts. Abstractly judged, such stakes might seem irrelevant to this inquiry: surely a classic must communicate on its own, apart from its author's personal relation to it. Yet a few lesser masterworks with strictly personal subtexts—Diderot's *Rameau's Nephew*, Chateaubriand's *René*, Constant's *Adolphe*, Strindberg's *To Damascus*—have found wide and continuing acceptance. Take *Adolphe*: perhaps its deft theme— that passion stales, then stale passion stifles—together with its probing prose suffice to assure its enduring appeal in spite of Constant's wholly self-centered subtext. After all, romanticism and expressionism both traded on personal confession in thinnest disguise. Can authors' secrets alone underpin at least minor classics?

Such secrets would need to do that underpinning alone: this much is clear from our sample dozen. For each classic studied has a single pervasive under-theme offsetting a single crucial overtheme. More, the two themes hold it together through their interaction. The exceptions that prove the rule in our sample are the old, primitive subtexts that survived vestigially in Sophocles' *Oedipus the King* and subordinately in Thomas's and Gottfried's Tristan sagas, overwritten in each by a new and more sophisticated substitute. Not in all its versions did the traditional legend that Sophocles dramatized end with Oedipus's banishment. Its original subtext, whether a Freudian father-and-mother complex or an exposed child's revenge, did not require it to; only Sophocles' new subtext, the traumatic reliving, did. Comparably, the hereditary trauma that Thomas superimposed on the Freudian family romance conspicuous beneath the received Tristan legend required Tristan's death in combat and then Isolde's death from grief where of itself that muffled Freudian motif could accommodate any punitive outcome whatever. Thus in both these cases the new undertexts dictated the dénouement. They also dictated countless passages of the Sophocles and then of the Thomas and the Gottfried that are unrelated to the old, residual subtexts, and they suffuse the full texts of the Greek tragedy and the medieval sagas as their received, residual subtexts do not. Hence these new subtexts are the dominant ones and can be regarded for present comparative purposes as *the* subtexts. Indeed, in every work or distinct episode of a work that I have analyzed here, as also for good measure in every other classic that I have explored the same way outside of the present twelvefold inquiry, a single subtext predominates even if other, lesser latent stuff mixes in.

At first blush it may appear nonetheless that the original subtext of the Tristan legend, having been invariant through all its sundry incarnations, alone accounts for its perennial appeal. Or again, the modern preference for Thomas's and Gottfried's like versions of Tristan's story may be attributed to their textual performances alone—to their poetic prowess, that is, or their dialectic of passion and sorrow—rather than, subtextually, to that fatal birthmark for which Thomas and then Gottfried had their Tristan named. The popularity of the core Tristan legend as distinct from any of its write-ups—the two ill-starred lovers embraced in effigy on household furniture and furnishings throughout late medieval Europe—might well weigh in for the old subtext again. So might the romantics' revival of the legend, after a couple of centuries' eclipse, with a premium on fated illicit passion. But the legend itself is not the issue here; only its classic rendition by Thomas and then Gottfried is. So are the relative weights of text and subtext beside my point, since a subtext requires a text and a classic requires both. To repeat, as here I may: a classic, to be one, needs a subtext to complement the text every stretch of the way. This is why the passage about the massacre of the innocents stands apart from Matthew's Gospel, the Francesca episode from Dante's poem, and the Inquisitor sequence from Dostoyevsky's novel, as self-contained: their subtexts begin and end where they do.[1] By the same token, if pieces of any loose-knit classic, such as Gottfried's sprawling *Tristan* or Shakespeare's prodigal *King Lear*, fit its text less than snugly, they fit its subtext too that much less than snugly.

With its parallel overtheme and undertheme, a classic is comparable to a dream composed out of a single dominant preconscious thought and a single dominant unconscious wish. However, unlike a text and its merely veiled subtext, the message of a dream on both these latent levels is encoded in archaic language requiring decipherment for even the dreamer to understand it after awakening. Besides, a subtext relates meaningfully to its text, unlike a latent to a manifest dream, or unconscious to preconscious dream material. Freud saw fiction as formalized daydreaming, itself analogous to dreaming proper. This is a flawed construction by Freud on his own sturdier dream theory. In this sturdier theory, a dream represents an unconscious, repressed infantile wish of the dreamer's as fulfilled while also expressing some preconscious thought or impulse that the dreamer has blocked or censored in the course of the previous day, all neatly disguised in ways that Freud nicely exposed. Daydreams resemble dreams proper except that their manifest content is closer to waking reality and invariably wishful—with, as Freud saw it, infantile input informing that wishing. Like a dream, a daydream is highly personal—and here the analogy with fiction possessing broad appeal fails at the very outset. For one man's or woman's wishful thinking is not normally another's, let alone universal and timeless. To say as Freud did that fictionists know how to depersonalize their daydreams is to sign off on his very premise, for daydreams are nothing if not personal. For that wide-awake wishing to come across literally, its infantile basis would likewise need to be widespread in the reading public at large, male and female alike, and then it would do nothing to explain why one work of fiction appeals while another does not.

The trouble with Freud's take on fiction is clearest when works of fiction are analyzed with an eye to their authorship and readership both. Witness our twelve classics: their concealed messages can in no case usefully be construed as unconscious wishing. True, the subtexts each tend to reconcile or resign us to the troubles dealt out in the texts, but such reconciling is a far cry from a joyride as in a daydream. God himself may be a wish fantasy, as Freud held, but the no-God in Dostoyevsky's subtext is no more wishful than God's bungled creation in Dostoyevsky's text. Similarly, that lust was built into Francesca's love, or that sin was inherent in Phaedra's, was no fond fancy for Dante or for Racine, let alone for us in reading them. Each subtext studied here, besides meeting with a universal and lasting response, presumably had special currency or resonance in its historic time, as did Dostoyevsky's subtext after Darwin had issued the Creator's death warrant, or again as did Mann's subtext at the height of Europe's artistic glamorization of death. *The Wild Duck* for its part belongs to a period when European fiction as a whole vented a powerful family hate subtextually. This rash of fictional family bashing spoke to no coincidence of personal wish fantasies, but to a widespread social and moral malaise.2 But again, this latent European malaise itself, however widespread, does not begin to explain which few period pieces concerned, including Ibsen's, became classics while so much other fiction to the same latent effect did not. That explanation must be sought instead within such classics themselves. So, leaving Freud to the Freudians, I return to my twelve specific classics, broken down into text and subtext, to explore what makes a classic a classic.

How do texts relate to subtexts in my twelve classics? This is far and away trickiest to say for *King Lear*, its initial setting being an unreality that text and subtext alike fast refute—a charmed never-never land that the text ravages from the start while the subtext keeps saying that it was never-never anyway. That initial setting is a make-believe Albion aglow with gentility. Already on square one a subjacent nastiness sounds through the initial sweet civility, then erupts so violently thereafter that Lear and Gloucester die of the shock effect, leaving their few survivors mortally stunned. Life, convulsion-prone in the text, is gangrened anyway in the subtext: like Lear's hand in Lear's own words toward the last, "it smells of mortality."3 But might not Lear, might not Gloucester and Edgar, have lived happily ever after, fairy-tale-like, on that serene square one had they just been less childishly gullible? No, the tragic text and subtext both agree: the halcyon initial setting, being unreal, could not hold. The text claims that we die of strange upsets; the subtext has it rather that, upsets or no, life is unlivable—that, in the text's own stark imagery, the deadly storm is the deadly norm. Hence each of the two, text and subtext, refutes the initial, make-believe theatrical conceit: this far they concur. But in addition—and this now cuts to the marrow—the subtext says no to the text.

This cuts to the marrow because the subtexts all say no to their texts, however variously. They all beg to differ. Does that "all" give pause? For memory, here are—encapsulated and schematized, and with apologies for such a trying listing—the dozen successive textual affirmations and subtextual rejoinders established piecemeal in the twelve chapters preceding. Fate ensnared Oedipus? No, Oedipus stampeded fate. Jesus atoned for our inborn guilt? No, for his own survivor guilt. Passion poisoned Tristan and Isolde? No, Tristan's tragic birth was their undoing. Francesca loved? No, she lusted. Life, if untroubled, ripens in olde England? No, it just rots. Forbidden love was Phaedra's curse? No, love itself was. Werther wasn't up to this world? No, this world wasn't up to Werther. Upstart Julien's false life was a freak? No, to live falsely is our common lot. Life passed simple Félicité by? No, hers was any and all life at its simplest. Christ, as per Dostoyevsky, bungled his first coming? No, a Christ never came. We must protect weak families like the Ekdals? No, for the family is what breeds weakness like the Ekdals'. Completing our dozen, Aschenbach chased after Tadzio and died? No, Aschenbach chased after his death by way of Tadzio. In each case the subtext contradicts the text, or undercuts it, or turns it topsy-turvy, but this in no wise definitively. On the contrary, the text preserves a total integrity on its own terms at the same time as on its underside it gives itself the lie.

This running negation *always* registers, however dimly. On Sophocles' stage we see how fate did Oedipus in, yet we sense equally that Oedipus tripped himself up. In Mann's pages we see how a plague and a Pole together undid Aschenbach, yet we feel too that Aschenbach was running a disaster course right from page one. The stories in between that first and last one all likewise hold exactly as told, yet each is also lined all the way by an inside counterstory putting a different spin on the selfsame yarn without which it would look flimsy and shoddy in due course, just like yesterday's bestsellers. Up to a crucial point, the interrelation of text and subtext, or outside and inside story, in these classics is like the one in quantum physics that Niels Bohr called "complementarity": each holds all the way even while logically the one excludes the other. The critical point at which this analogy breaks down is that in "complementarity," unlike text and subtext, neither of the two mutually exclusive readings of a given phenomenon is more immediate or more apparent, or conversely more hidden or elusive, than the other. On the face of it, light is no more waves than particles, no more particles than waves. Oedipus, however, is more obviously trapped by Apollo than traumatized, and Aschenbach manifestly more smitten with Tadzio than with death. But again and yet again, neither the outer nor the inner story ever gains, let alone holds, a clear edge. Uncertainty is the name of the game twelve times over.

The form of each classic analyzed tends to accord with the sense of its subtext as well as with the sense of its text even though these two senses themselves are forever at odds. Thus Sophocles' play is styled as a ritual replay, with Oedipus's three traumatic moments conflated into a single spectacle. Thus too Matthew's Gospel skips diptychlike straight from baby Jesus' "innocent crime" to grown-up Jesus' message of salvation and act of atonement. Thomas's and Gottfried's singsong rhythms and rhymes, their refrains and redundancies, resonate with their undertheme of fated reliving. Lust enfolds Francesca in the architectonics of Dante's *Inferno* even as she professes love. *King Lear* rushes headlong from its fablelike start into baroque chaos pending the final calm of exhaustion. The universalizing idiom of Racine's classicism downright required Phaedra's indomitable sin to be not just her own specific unworthy love, but love as such. Goethe's would-be cautionary case history of a suicide set that passionate suicide up to speak for itself. *The Red and the Black* is tied to its scheming hero's continual self-deception only to wind up turning this fatal course into a formula for the human lot. Flaubert's reductive style lowered all human existence to the level of a humble heroine designed to quintessentialize it. Dostoyevsky's vehicle for his subtextual denial of Christ's reality was a fable featuring a tangible Christ. Ibsen constructed his textual case for protective lies around a fake forest harboring a plumply degenerate wild duck snug in a cozy basket. And Mann cast his account of death-ridden Aschenbach's encounter with his fate about like an inner monologue.

Though the same form suits them both in each case, text and subtext never reconcile. Their contrariety even intensifies as each work progresses. Sophocles' Oedipus relives his formative infantile exposure even in doing as the oracle said he would do. Matthew's Jesus fulfills prophecies even in expiating his guilt to the hilt. Thomas's Tristan dies lovelorn for Isolde even in dying his father's death. Francesca's profession of love draws telltale tears of remorse from Paolo. Strange mutations prevent life from mellowing in *King Lear* even as this preventing would also be life's normal way—"the rack of this tough world."[4] Phaedra's folly is fueled by the goddess of love. Werther's alienation peaks at beguiling lyric heights. Julien's destiny goes the limit in strangeness only to symbolize our mortal fate. Félicité is closest to our common human core in her uncommon simplicity. The Inquisitor's grievances against Christ also refute Christ's existence. Not even with Hedvig's suicide does the textual case for the "life-lie" in *The Wild Duck* gain a momentary edge, what with portentous Old Ekdal on hand to mumble and remumble about the forest's revenge. Finally, Tadzio beckoning in Aschenbach's dying vision points equally to love and to death. Only *Oedipus the King* may seem to privilege its subtext insofar as fate, its textual mainstay, does not foil Oedipus during the play itself, but has already run him to ground conclusively half a lifetime before. However, the criminal investigation commanded by Apollo aptly mimics fate on stage, assuming a momentum of its own the more it closes in on Oedipus despite his running resistance at the same time that he plies it to his traumatic purpose with mounting frenzy. Like the other twelvefold patterns noted, this one of running contrariety holds equally whether the subtext glares right through the textual surface or hides deep down below it.

By now we are ready to abstract from our specimen classics. On their evidence a classic tells, and supremely well, a tale with a sharp point to it that it meanwhile also implicitly rejects. Its sharp point and matching, muted counterpoint shape it overall: thence its felt unity. The polarity is never resolved between the two rival morals of the classic tale, the one express and the other tacit, the one outspoken and the other whispered, the one affirmed and the other insinuated: thence its ambiguity, its felt depth, its enduring vitality. Overtheme and undertheme are cross-fertile contraries, like a male and a female principle that play off each other until they climax together. Both besides tend to universality in the process. Or more fully stated: the main characters of a classic work, however singularized, are figures for humanity at large contending with ultimates—God, fate, love, life, death, guilt, authenticity, belonging. This universalist pitch carries even where, as in *The Red and the Black*, it comes into the open only at the climax itself to pull the work together retroactively and catapult it to classic heights. Possibly some nonclassics have filled that same bill in full, though I can discover none now. Possibly too, classics other than my twelve are not all shaped by a conflicting theme and subtheme, so that my abstracting from twelve classics, however representative they may be, will not hold up beyond that small sample itself. But I chose my twelve with no advance hint of these findings—which, obvious as they may look by now, I took embarrassingly long to reach even after my monographic chapters were all written and rewritten. So to my mind they bid fair to speak for their kind.

If they do speak for their kind, then classics consist of texts and dissenting subtexts about the same ultimates and push their two claims at variance every inch of the way. Of course a work that fills this bill is not ipso facto a classic: mess up the rhymes in *Phaedra* and it will lapse from the canon. But to fill that double bill is for a classic as much of a must as the aesthetic must: *Esther's* alexandrines match *Phaedra's*, but *Esther* with its single-tier, Sunday-school moral would never have survived its author except that he also wrote *Phaedra*. That classics deal in human fundamentals, however markedly of their time and place some classics are, should surprise no one in view of their wide and lasting appeal. Lasting, by the way, does not mean stable: Tristan sat out the Enlightenment, and Stendhal's "chronicle of 1830" took a half-century or more to catch on. No classic's appeal is ever unanimous either, or even as great at its peak as is the lure of so much ephemeral matter. Part of the reason why the public for classics is small at any one time or place is no doubt that very tension between text and subtext that also keeps classics alive. For fundamentals are no fun to face; still less, then, is a story about them that undermines its own ostensible message. In the popular medieval forms of the Tristan legend, love was a fatal curse, period; by adding Tristan's tragic birth sub rosa as an alternative fatal curse, Thomas and then Gottfried turned a medieval Europe-wide favorite into an epic marvel for the happy, or more likely unhappy, few. No matter that their verse is eminently simple and inexhaustibly rich: deathless it is, but hardly popular.

So a classic second-guesses itself, is divided against itself, internally. What then of elite culture, where the classics have their home? Scholars have lately taken to speaking of elite culture with a plebeian sneer as a fringe effect, a mere emanation and refinement of mass culture. However, to judge by the classics as contrasted with pulp fiction, the difference lies not in degrees of subtlety or fastidiousness in working up our common human experience, but rather in the elites' acquired tolerance or even taste for uncertainty. This would be a true and a deep divide however commonly it is crossed.

NOTES

1. This is also why Degas's hidden-image *Steep Coast*, cited at the outset, is not fully analogous to a literary classic with its text and subtext: the camouflaged nude covers only the middle third of the canvas.

2. See my "Fiction as Social Fantasy: Europe's Domestic Crisis of 1879–1914," *Journal of Social History* 27, no. 4 (Summer 1994): 679–99.

3. Shakespeare, *King Lear*, IV.vi.132.

4. Ibid., V.iii.313.

Index

Adultery: extraneous, 47, 51; a felt duty, 95; hurtful, 40–41; taints its issue, 60–61; a vile craving, 71, 74, 77

Aeneid (Virgil), 24–25

Aeschylus, 18; *Agamemnon*, 11, 18; *Choephoroe*, 18; *Oresteia*, 18, 25

Agamemnon (Aeschylus), 11, 18

Andreyev, Leonid, *Story of Seven Who Were Hanged*, 102 n.23

Antigone (Sophocles), 4, 7

Appearances, false, 56, 58, 62

Aristotle, 1, 19 n.6, 72, 78 n.4

Arrival and Departure (Koestler), 26

Art, 28–29, 31 nn.27–29, 45, 53, 82, 130, 140

Auerbach, Erich, *Mimesis*, 5

Authorial absence, Flaubert's, 108

Authorial presence: and ambivalence, 81, 84–86, 89–90, 119–21; Dostoyevsky's, 120; Goethe's, 5, 89–90; Stendhal's, 93, 96; in subtexts, 146

The Bacchae (Euripides), 4

Balzac, Honoré de, 94–95; *Eugénie Grandet*, 94; *The Human Comedy*, 94; *Lost Illusions*, 94; *Old Goriot*, 94

Barna da Siena, 28

Baroque, 2, 73, 150

Baudelaire, Charles, 144 n.20

Bergson, Henri, 4

Béroul, 34, 40, 42–43 n.19

Bildungsroman, 89

Black Death, 29

Boccaccio, Giovanni, 45

Bohr, Niels, 150

Boileau, Nicolas, 78 n.4

Boswell, James, 85

Bouvard and Pécuchet (Flaubert), 104

The Breakdown (Dürrenmatt), 99

The Brothers Karamazov (Dostoyevsky), 113

Büchner, Georg, 99, 101; *Danton's Death*, 98
Buff, Charlotte, 84, 85

Cain, 54 n.10
Camus, Albert, *The Fall*, 24–26; *The Stranger*, 99–100
Canon, 152–53. *See also* Classics
Charon, 140
The Charterhouse of Parma (Stendhal), 101
Chateaubriand, François-René de, *René*, 146
Choephoroe (Aeschylus), 18
Christ: abets adultery, 40; guilt-ridden, 21–30, 145, 149–51; left humans mortal, 97; revisits mankind, 114–20, 146, 149–51
Christianity: a cultural phase, 137; a deliverance, 88; a divine scandal, 113–21; humanized, 28–30; no option, 97–98; punitive, 45, 52–53; severe, 73, 75, 77–78
Classicism: along Aschenbach's regressive way, 137; in Flaubert's subtext, 110; Racine at its height, 72–73, 75, 150; the romantics' bugbear, 94; universalizes, 75, 110, 150
Classics: appeal of, 1, 3, 152–53; nature of, 1, 3–4, 145–53; sampled, 2, 3, 145; and ultimates, 152. *See also* Canon; Text and subtext; Text and subtext, interrelation of
Cocteau, Jean, 130
"Complementarity," 150
Constant, Benjamin, *Adolphe*, 146

Dante Alighieri, 116, 146; *Inferno* (from *The Divine Comedy*), 45–53, 72, 145–51
Danton's Death (Büchner), 98
Darkness at Noon (Koestler), 99
Darwin, Charles, 125, 128, 148

Death: eroticized, 40, 88, 139, 145; glamorized, 148
Death in Venice (Mann), 135–46, 148–51
Death row, 97–101
Deathwatch (Genet), 99
Death wish, 73, 88, 129, 132, 139–43, 144 n.46, 145
Degas, Edgar, 2, 153 n.1
Descartes, René, 4, 73
Dictionary of Received Ideas (Flaubert), 109
Diderot, Denis, *Rameau's Nephew*, 146
Dionysus, 137, 140, 142
Doctor Faustus (Marlowe), 97, 120
Don Quixote (Cervantes), 3
Dostoyevsky, Fyodor, 119–21, 146; *The Brothers Karamazov*, 113, 120; "The Grand Inquisitor," 113–21, 146–51
Dreams, 2, 128, 137, 140–42, 148–49
Durkheim, Émile, Ibsen's approach like his, 130
Dürrenmatt, Friedrich: *The Breakdown*, 99; *The Visit*, 99

Eckermann, Johann Peter, 85
Eilhart von Oberge, 34, 40, 42–43
Elijah, 23
Entropy, 65–66
Eugénie Grandet (Balzac), 94
Euripides, 18; *The Bacchae*, 4; *Hippolytus*, 71–72, 74–77; *Ion*, 19 n.28; *The Trojan Women*, 25
Expressionism, 139–42, 146

The Fall (Camus), 24–26
Family hate, 148–49
Fate: as classic theme, 152; and form, 75, 77, 140, 150
Fate, ways of: brewed, 34, 36–40, 147; instinctual-regressive, 138–40, 151; lusty, 52; oracular, 7–8, 18, 150–51; prophetic, 27; venereal, 75, 77

Flaubert, Gustave, 3, 107, 146; *Bou-
    vard and Pécuchet*, 104; *Dictionary
    of Received Ideas*, 109; "Herodias,"
    108; *Madame Bovary*, 104; "Saint
    Julian Hospitator," 108; "A Simple
    Heart," 103–11, 146, 149–51;
    Three Tales, 108
Florio, John, 58
Form and fate, 75, 77, 140, 150
Form and subtext, 150–51
Form and text/subtext: in Dante, 49,
    52; in Flaubert, 108–9; in Ibsen,
    132; in *Lear*, 57, 66, 72; in Mann,
    135, 139–40; in *Phaedra*, 72, 77–
    78; in Stendhal, 98; in *Werther*, 90
Franco, Francisco, 99
Frederick the Great, 136–37
French Revolution, 94–96
Freud, Sigmund: on death wish, 143,
    144 n.46; on dreams, 148–49;
    Goethe's approach unlike his, 89;
    Ibsen's approach like his, 130; and
    Sophocles, 4–5, 7–8, 17–18, 20
    n.47, 33–34; on subtexts, 5
Freudian complex: alias Oedipus com-
    plex, 5; maybe Oedipus's original
    subtext, 33, 146–47; misfits Sopho-
    cles' play, 7–8; reflects Sophocles'
    play Freudianly, 17; Tristan's origi-
    nal subtext, 33–36, 147; behind
    Werther's love, 91 n.20

Genet, Jean, *Deathwatch*, 99
Goethe, Johann Wolfgang, 81–90,
    137, 145–46; and *Bildungsroman*,
    89; "mirroring" in novels, 83, 85–
    86; *The Sorrows of Young Werther*,
    5, 81–91, 96, 120, 145–46, 149–
    51; *Wilhelm Meister's Apprentice-
    ship*, 85, 89
Gottfried von Strassburg, *Tristan*, 33–
    44, 69 n.129, 77, 89, 145–50, 152
Grace: necessary for salvation, 73; of-
    fered by Christ, 97; spurned by In-
quisitor, 114–15, 117; unavailable
    to pagan Phaedra, 75; unwanted by
    Julien, 98
"The Grand Inquisitor" (Dos-
    toyevsky), 113–21, 146–51
Gray, Ronald, 130
Guilt: ancient, 25; Christian, 149; clas-
    sic, 152; erotic, 73, 75, 77–78; exis-
    tential, 99–100; hereditary, 73–74;
    in Julien, 97; in Oedipus, 17; in
    Phaedra, 73; in Tristan and Isolde,
    40–41
Guilt trap, 74

Han of Iceland (Hugo), 97
Henry IV (Pirandello), 18
Herod, 21–24, 27–28
"Herodias" (Flaubert), 108
Herodotus, 25
Hidden-image painting, 1–2, 153 n.1
Hippolytus (Euripides), 71–72, 74–77
Holocaust, 26
Homer, 137; *The Iliad*, 21; *The Odys-
    sey*, 23–25
Hugo, Victor: *Han of Iceland*, 97; *The
    Last Day of a Condemned Man*, 97–
    98, 100
The Human Comedy (Balzac), 94

Ibsen, Henrik, 123, 126; *Little Eyolf*,
    18, 20 n.49; *The Wild Duck*, 123–
    34, 146, 148–49, 151
Identity (personal), unstable in *Lear*,
    59–65
The Iliad (Homer), 21
Incest: craved, 71, 74–75, 77; unwit-
    ting, 8–15; vicarious, 34–36
Inferno (Dante), 45–54, 72, 145–51
Ingres, Dominique, 53
Invitation to a Beheading (Nabokov), 99
Ion (Euripides), 19 n.28

Jansenism, 73–74, 77
Jeremiah, 22, 24, 29

Jerusalem, Carl Wilhelm, 84–86, 88
Jesus. *See* Christ
Josephus, 23

Kafka, Franz, *The Trial*, 99
Kestner, Johann Christian, 84–85, 90
    n.9
King Lear (Shakespeare), 3–4, 17, 55–
    69, 72, 146–47, 149–51
Koestler, Arthur: *Arrival and Depar-
    ture*, 26; *Darkness at Noon*, 99;
    Spanish Testament, 102 n.29

Lancelot, 46, 48–50
La Roche, Maximiliane von, 90 n.4
La Roche, Sophie von, 90 n.4
The Last Day of a Condemned Man
    (Hugo), 97–98, 100
Lincoln, Abraham, 25, 29
Little Eyolf (Ibsen), 18, 20 n.49
Lost Illusions (Balzac), 94
Louis XIV, 72, 137
Love: and death, 36–41, 47, 50–52,
    54 n.4, 74–76, 88, 98, 139, 142,
    145; and sin, 51–53, 75–78, 148,
    150; and society, 40–41, 77, 95–96
Love, modes of: Aschenbach's suicidal,
    137, 139–43; Christ's indiscrimi-
    nate, 114, 116–17; Félicité's self-
    less, 103–4, 106, 110; Francesca's
    wicked, 47–53; Hedvig's sacrificial,
    129; Hjalmar's pathetic, 124–25;
    Julien's unstable, 95–96, 98; Lear's
    imperious, 4, 56, 61–63; Madame
    de Rênal's pure, 98; Mathilde's
    heady, 95; Phaedra's a scourge, 71–
    81; Tristan's and Isolde's fatal, 36–
    41; Werther's sterile, 81–90

Macpherson, James, 82
Madame Bovary (Flaubert), 104

Mann, Thomas, 145; *Death in Venice*,
    135–46, 148–51; vs. Freud on
    death drive, 144 n.46
Mark, Gospel of, 22, 26
Marlowe, Christopher, *Doctor Faustus*,
    97
Marx, Karl, 88
Mary, 22, 28–29, 31 n.23
Massacre of the innocents, 21–31
Matthew, 22; Gospel of, 21–31, 145,
    147, 149–51
Method, 4
Mimesis (Auerbach), 5
Montaigne, Michel de, 58–59, 67 n.43
Montserrat (Roblès), 99
Moses, 23, 25, 53
Murder: bungled by Julien, 93–98; en-
    chanted in Genet, 99; fantasized by
    Phaedra, 77; foretold in *Oedipus*, 7,
    9, 13–17; replayed in *Oresteia*, 18;
    shameful in *Othello*, 65; unmeaning
    in Camus, 99; unsisterly in *Lear*,
    62; untimely in Dante, 46–47, 51,
    54 n.10; vindicated by Werther, 83,
    85–87; wholesale in Mathew, 22–29
Murphy, James, 20 n.47
Music, 18, 45
Mutations, 55–60

Nabokov, Vladimir, *Invitation to a
    Beheading*, 99
Napoleon Bonaparte, 93
Narcissus, 139
Naturalism, 78, 130, 132
Nietzsche, Friedrich, 100–101, 125
No Exit (Sartre), 18

The Odyssey (Homer), 23–25
Oedipus at Colonus (Sophocles), 18
Oedipus complex, 5, 7–8, 17, 33–36,
    147

Oedipus the King (Sophocles): misread by Freud, 4–5, 7–8, 34; read right, 8–20, 34, 39, 145–47, 149–51

Oedipus legend: familiar beyond words, 16; known as myth, 27; oft-told, 18; recalled in *Tristan*, 43 n.25; subtext likely an exposed child's revenge, 8, 147; subtext maybe once Freudian, 33, 147; variants rejected by Sophocles, 15, 18

Oresteia (Aeschylus), 18, 25

Ossian, 82

Othello (Shakespeare), 65

Pandarus, 54 n.7

Pascal, Blaise, 73, 97–99

Paul (apostle), 22, 26, 99

Pericles, 25

Petrarch, Francis, 29–30

Phaedra (Racine), 4, 71–79, 89, 146, 148–52

Pietà, 29–30, 31 n.28

Pirandello, Luigi: *Henry IV*, 18; *Six Characters in Search of an Author*, 18

Platen, August von, 137, 141

Plutarch, 137

Poetics: Aristotle's, 19 n.6, 72, 78 n.4; Boileau's, 78 n.4

Preplay, 10–11

Prudentius, 28

Rachel, 22, 24–25, 29, 30 n.14, 31 n.29

Racine, Jean, 71–72, 76, 94, 110; *Esther*, 152; *Phaedra*, 4, 71–79, 89, 146, 148–52

Realism, 103–6, 108–9, 130

The Red and the Black (Stendhal), 2, 89, 93–102, 146, 149–52

René (Chateaubriand), 146

Róbert, Friar, 42 n.7

Roblès, Emmanuel, *Montserrat*, 99

Romanticism, 2–3, 93–96, 98–99, 120, 146–47

Rousseau, Jean-Jacques, 94, 96

"Saint Julian Hospitator" (Flaubert), 108

Sartre, Jean-Paul: *No Exit*, 18; "The Wall," 99–100

Schiller, Friedrich, 136

Sebastian, Saint, 137

Shakespeare, William, 3, 57–59, 145; *King Lear*, 3–4, 17, 55–69, 72, 146–47, 149–51; *Othello*, 65; *The Tempest*, 69 n.128

Shame: in antiquity, 25; behind fictional suicides, 139; from failed ambition, 95; over base passion, 73–74; over love, 74; over sex, 95; upon going gay, 137

"A Simple Heart" (Flaubert), 103–11, 146, 149–51

Sin: beats out virtue, 4, 75, 110; carnal variety defined, 48–49; Christ's subtextual, 31 n.24; Francesca's unavowed, 46–53; licensed by Inquisitor, 114–15; Phaedra's universal, 4, 75, 77, 148, 150; relived forever if unrepented, 45–46; sinners' stock spin on, 49; Werle's familial, 126

Six Characters in Search of an Author (Pirandello), 18

Socrates, 137

Sophocles, 4, 7–8, 18, 72; *Antigone*, 4, 7; *Oedipus at Colonus*, 18–19; *Oedipus the King*, 4–5, 7–20, 25, 27–28, 33, 39, 145–47, 149–51

The Sorrows of Young Werther (Goethe), 5, 81–91, 96, 120, 146, 149–51

Spain, 3, 99–100, 102 n.29

Spanish Testament (Koestler), 102 n.29

Spielrein, Sabina, 144 n.46

Stein, Charlotte von, 85, 91 n.20

Stendhal, Henri Beyle, 3, 93–95, 99, 101, 101 n.18; *The Charterhouse of Parma*, 101; *The Red and the Black*, 2–3, 89, 93–102, 146, 149–52

Story of Seven Who Were Hanged (Andreyev), 102 n.23

The Stranger (Camus), 99–100

Strauss, Leo, 4

Strindberg, August, 125; *To Damascus*, 146; *A Dream Play*, 141

Subtext, 1–4, 10–11; can dictate dénouement, 147; conveyed indirectly as a rule, 90; and form, 150–51; may be personal, 146; may evolve in myths, 32–36, 146–47; more or less veiled, 4, 151; one per classic, 3, 146–47; rationalizes textual ills, 145–46. *See also* Text and subtext; Text and subtext, interrelation of

Suicide: committed in Goethe, 81–89, 150; committed in Ibsen, 124, 126, 129, 132; committed in Racine, 74–75; committed in Shakespeare, 62; committed in Sophocles, 9–10, 15; thwarted in Shakespeare, 55, 60; uncommitted in Ibsen, 129; virtual in Mann, 139

Surrealism, 99

Survivor guilt, 23–26, 29–30, 31 nn.23, 24, 149

Symbols: baroque, 2; in Flaubert, 109–10; in Goethe, 89–90; in Ibsen, 126–28, 130–32; in Mann, 140–43; in Racine, 75–77; in Stendhal, 100; in Tristan legend, 34, 36–38

Tacitus, *Germania*, 42 n.5

The Tempest (Shakespeare), 69 n.128

Text and subtext: analogized, 1–2, 148–50; coextensive, 3–4, 146–49; contrary, 149–52; distinguished, 1–4. *See also* Form and subtext; Form

and text/subtext; Subtext; Text and subtext, interrelation of

Text and subtext, interrelation of, 146–52; Dante, 52; Dostoyevsky, 120; Flaubert, 106, 110; Ibsen, 126, 129, 131–32; *Lear,* 66; Mann, 138–39, 143; Matthew, 27–29; *Oedipus,* 18, 27; *Phaedra,* 77–78; Stendhal, 98; Tristan, 39; *Werther,* 86, 89–90. *See also* Form and subtext; Form and text/subtext; Subtext; Text and subtext

Thomas of Britain, *Tristran,* 33–44, 77, 89, 145–47, 149–52

Three Tales (Flaubert), 108

Traumatic reliving, 7–8, 10, 12–14, 18, 20, n.49; blood for blood, 26–29, 31 n.23, 34, 145, 149; exposure as self-exposure, 7–18, 28, 34; like father, like son, 28, 33–34

The Trial (Kafka), 99

Tristan (Gottfried), 33–44, 69 n.129, 77, 89, 145–47, 149–52

Tristan legend, 5, 33–44, 50, 54 n.12

Tristran (Thomas), 33–44, 77, 89, 145–47, 149–52

The Trojan Women (Euripides), 25

Uncertainty, 58, 150, 153

Unities, three dramatic, 72–73, 75

Vigny, Alfred de, 98

Virgil, 45–46, 48, 50, 137; *Aeneid,* 24–25, 54 n.4

The Visit (Dürrenmatt), 99

Voltaire, François-Marie Arouet de, 136

Wagner, Richard, 40

"The Wall" (Sartre), 99–100

The Wild Duck (Ibsen), 123–34, 146, 148–49, 151

Wittgenstein, Ludwig, 2

World War I, 3, 99

Xenophon, 137

About the Author

RUDOLPH BINION is Leff Professor of History at Brandeis University. He is the author of numerous works including *Hitler Among the Germans* (1976) and *Love Beyond Death* (1993).

DATE DUE

GAYLORD			PRINTED IN U.S.A.